A Pictorial Guide to
the Military Museums, Forts,
and Historic Sites
of the United States

Also by James B. Sweeney

A PICTORIAL HISTORY OF OCEANOGRAPHIC SUBMERSIBLES

A PICTORIAL HISTORY OF SEA MONSTERS
AND OTHER DANGEROUS MARINE LIFE

A Pictorial Guide to the Military Museums, Forts, and Historic Sites of the United States

by

James B. Sweeney
Lt. Col. USAF (Ret.)

CROWN PUBLISHERS, INC.   NEW YORK

Inquiries should be addressed to Crown Publishers, Inc., One Park
Avenue, New York, New York 10016

Printed in the United States of America

Published simultaneously in Canada by General Publishing Company Limited

Library of Congress Cataloging in Publication Data

Sweeney, James B.
A pictorial guide to the military museums, forts, and historic sites of the United States.

1. Military museums—United States. I. Title.
U13.U6S694 1981   069′.9355′0973   81-3291
ISBN:0-517-544814   AACR2

10 9 8 7 6 5 4 3 2 1

First Edition

This book is dedicated to:

Dr. Frank J. Sweeney
Dr. James M. Sweeney
Dr. John R. Sweeney

CONTENTS

Part II. Sea Museums

Part III. Air Museums

Part IV. Overseas Museums

Maj. Gen. Francis S. Greenlief, Ret.
Executive Vice-President, National Guard Association of
the United States

FOREWORD

by

Major General Francis S. Greenlief, Ret.

History, which is the process by which man passes along to his successors an understanding of how he lived, is recorded in many different ways. It is found in printed pages of books and journals. It is passed along by word of mouth. In more recent times it has been recorded for posterity on magnetic tape and videotape.

It has long seemed to me that of all the ways in which history is preserved, the medium of the museum is, by far and away, the most meaningful for the greatest number of people. The museum raises the depiction of history to its highest level in terms of truth and factuality; it reduces the requirement for viewer involvement to the simple willingness to look.

Because what it shows, for the most part, consists of actual artifacts of a specific and definable character, the content of a museum is not susceptible to challenge, to charges of editorial bias or to misinterpretation. The contents of a museum are explicit. Seeing something in three-dimensional reality has lasting impact—whether the object is a 19th-century Gatling gun or a package of World War II rations.

The military museum is a very special contribution to the nation's history. This pictorial tour of "Military Museums, Forts, and Historic Sites of the United States"—the author's phrase which reflects the subject matter of this volume—links the American of today with the glory, the grandeur, and even the grim moments of our great country's evolution from struggling colonies to superpower.

General Greenlief is the executive director of The Historical Society of the Militia and National Guard, which operates the National Guard Heritage Gallery in Washington, D.C. The gallery, which opened its doors July 4, 1976, contains a valuable collection of militia and National Guard artifacts. He served in the Pentagon from January 1960 until his retirement from active status on July 1, 1974.

General Greenlief was born in Hastings, Nebraska, and was enrolled in the University of Nebraska when his unit was mobilized in December 1940. As a platoon leader and later company commander, he took part in the Normandy, Northern France, Rhineland, and Ardennes campaigns. He rejoined the Nebraska Army National Guard after his release from active duty in January 1946. By July 1957, he had risen to the rank of Colonel. Accepting an active-duty tour in the National Guard Bureau, he took on a series of responsible posts culminating in his appointment as Chief, National Guard Bureau on September 1, 1971. He is an Army aviator, wears the Combat Infantry Badge and his decorations include both the Army and the Air Force Distinguished Service Medal. He holds the Silver Star and a Purple Heart with three Oak-Leaf Clusters.

PREFACE

This book is divided into three main sections: Land (museums dealing with ground action), Sea (museums dealing with military nautical matters), and Air (museums dealing with aviation combat). In making these divisions, I have kept in mind that the Army has numerous aircraft, the Air Force has a great many seagoing vessels, the Navy has thousands of land-oriented troops, and the National Guard a massive collection of assorted weapons. The traditional Army, Navy, Air Force, Coast Guard, and National Guard distinctions are no longer steadfast when it comes to museums.

Within each section the book is arranged alphabetically by state and, within states, by city.

Many of this nation's finest military museums are known by other names—historic parks, memorials, visitor centers, sites, battlefields, forts, and replicas. All house a collection of military artifacts and memorabilia, and each institution listed in this book has something soldierly to be seen. None has been picked at random; all have been carefully selected, screened, and questioned. In this regard, special thanks is due the following for their assistance in checking accuracy of content: Maj. H. G. Jessup; Sgt. George Carroll; Dr. Norman Carey; Rear Adm. F. H. Miller, USN; Mrs. Alice B. Price; Capt. Rick DuCharme, USAF; Mr. Dana Bell; Mr. Fred R. Bell: Miss Mishi Kamiya; Mr. Chuck Haberlein; Lt. Col. Robert Henderson, Jr.; Cal L. Traylor; and many other wonderful people.

Part I

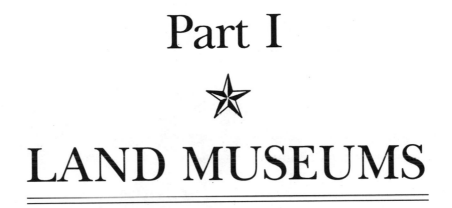

LAND MUSEUMS

FORT GAINES AND CONFEDERATE MUSEUM

Dauphin Island, AL 36528

Hours: Daily 9 A.M. to dusk

Cost of admission: Nominal charge

Description: Historic Fort Gaines and Confederate Museum, located 30 miles south of Mobile, Ala., on Dauphin Island, was established in 1821 for the defense of Mobile Bay. The fort is named for Gen. Edmund Gaines, who captured Aaron Burr while he was commander of the fort. Former "officers' quarters" building is now a museum, but there are many other things to see in the fort itself. There is a large bakery with giant ovens and storerooms; tunnels; gun emplacements; blacksmith shops; powder magazines; quartermaster offices; orderly room; and commandant's office, plus numerous additional sites of historic interest.

Historic Fort Gaines, located 30 miles south of Mobile, Ala., on Dauphin Island, was established in 1821 for the defense of Mobile Bay.

Located on Gun Hill is this 6-pounder and a smaller 3-pounder cannon. From this hill on March 27, 1814, Gen. Andrew Jackson directed the bombardment of the Indian barricade several hundred yards to the front with similar cannon.

One of the walls overlooking beautiful Mobile Bay. Fort Gaines is named for Gen. Edmund Pendleton Gaines who captured Aaron Burr while he was commander of the fort.

HORSESHOE BEND NATIONAL MILITARY PARK

Rt. 1, Box 103, Daviston, AL 36256
Telephone: (205) 234-7111 or 329-9905
Superintendent: Walter T. Bruce; Curator: Paul Ghioto
Hours: Daily 8 A.M. to 4:30 P.M.
Cost of admission: Free to the public
Description: The park and its museum, on Ala. 49, is 12 miles north of Dadeville and 18 miles northeast of Alexander City via Newsite. The park's museum contains artifacts of the Creek Indian War of 1813–14, which the Battle of Horseshoe Bend ended; also, artifacts dug up from the Indian village sites of Tohopeka and Nuyauka, which are within park boundaries and played roles in the battle. Military weapons of the period are also on display. Temporary exhibits are also set up from time to time dealing with park history.

Horseshoe Bend National Military Park is part of the National Park Service, U.S. Department of the Interior. Visitors to the park can explore the past by visiting the museum and driving along the tour road through the historic battlefield.

MILITARY POLICE CORPS MUSEUM

Bldg. 3182, Fort McClellan, AL 36205
Telephone: (205) 238-3522
Curator: Scott L. Norton
Hours: Daily 8 A.M. to 4 P.M.; closed weekends and holidays
Cost of admission: Free to the public
Description: Fort McClellan is 1 mile northeast of Anniston. From I-59 take Rt. 431 east (near Gadsden) 41 miles to Anniston. In Anniston turn left at Rt. 21; 1 mile to Fort McClellan. Museum contains history and artifacts of the U.S. Army Military Police serving throughout the world. Collection includes photographs, documents, colors, guidons, decorations, uniforms, U.S. and foreign weapons. Confiscated criminal apparatus is also included in collection. Of special meaning is a pair of crossed Harpers Ferry pistols, from which the Military Police Corps adapted their insignia. Uniforms on display date back to the Revolutionary War.

This case (between flags) contains a pair of crossed Harpers Ferry pistols from which the MP Corps takes its insignia. The Military Police Corps is one of the youngest branches of the Army. It was established on September 26, 1941. Its traditions of duty and service, however, are unsurpassed in our armed services. Soldiers have been performing police duties from the time of the Revolutionary War, when these duties were assigned mainly to a mounted police force. Soldiers serving as the Veteran's Reserve Corps and Provost Corps performed military police duties during the Civil War. MPs served with distinction in the Spanish-American War, World War I, World War II, the Korean War, and in Vietnam. As a result of hard work and distinguished service, the Military Police Corps was designated a combat support arm and service of the Army on October 14, 1968.

Military Police from the Revolutionary War to the present.

American MPs escort POWs (World War I).

German POWs with casualty under guard by MP (World War II).

WOMEN'S ARMY CORPS MUSEUM

Bldg. 1077, Fort McClellan, AL 36205
Telephone: (205) 238-3512
Acting Curator: Miss Gabriele E. Lorony
Hours: Daily 8 A.M. to 4 P.M.; closed holidays
Cost of admission: Free to the public

Description: Fort McClellan is 1 mile northeast of Anniston. From I-59 take Rt. 431 east (near Gadsden) 41 miles to Anniston. In Anniston turn left at Rt. 21; 1 mile to Baltzell Gate, Fort McClellan. The Women's Army Corps (WAC) Museum is in Building 1077. Artifacts depict history of the Women's Army Corps, including the Women's Army Auxiliary Corps (WAAC) from which it descends. On display is a collection of uniforms, flags, guidons, sheet music, recruiting posters, and personal memorabilia. Also on hand is a large collection of photographs and albums documenting the role of women in the U.S. military. Building contains a minitheater with numerous films from history through today's integrated training.

At the 14th Port, Southampton, England, a group of U.S. Army WACs board a troop transport, via gangplank, on their way to France, July 15, 1944. D-Day was June 6, 1944. WACs landed at Normandy Beach on D + 38.

Building 1077, WAC Museum, Fort McClellan, Ala.

U.S. ARMY AVIATION MUSEUM

Fort Rucker, AL 36362
Telephone: (205) 255-4507 or 255-4516
Curator: Thomas J. Sabiston
Hours: Monday through Friday 9 A.M. to 4 P.M.;
weekends and holidays 1 P.M. to 5 P.M.; closed
Christmas
Cost of admission: Free to the public
Description: Fort Rucker is 60 miles south of Montgomery. From Rt. 231, take Rt. 134 west (near Ozark) 5 miles to main gate. The Aviation Museum collects, preserves, restores, and displays aircraft, artifacts, documents, and other items that tell the story of Army aviation. Numerous military aircraft are on exhibit, including the largest collection of military helicopters in any museum in the world. The museum also has a large collection of documentary research materials relating to Army aviation.

Part of the largest collection of military helicopters in the world.

1/L-20A Utility (U-6 Beaver) airplane.

7

FORT MORGAN MUSEUM

Star Rt. Box 2780
Gulf Shores, AL 36542
Telephone: (205) 540-7125 or 540-7127
Acting Curator: Jane M. McDonald
Hours: Daily 8 A.M. to 5 P.M.; closed Thanksgiving, Christmas, and New Year's Day
Cost of admission: Free to the public
Description: Mobile Point, the site of Fort Morgan, is at the end of a scenic drive 22 miles from Gulf Shores, with the Gulf of Mexico on one side and Mobile Bay on the other. Fort Morgan, considered one of the finest examples of brick architecture in America, was designed by Simon Bernard, a French engineer and former aide-de-camp to Napoleon.

Flags flying over Fort Morgan's entrance reflect its long history and the many changes in the area. Before the first explorers sailed into Mobile Bay, Indians in dugout canoes plied the rivers and bays, seeking seafood. They left behind bits of pottery and arrowheads.

The museum contains military artifacts from the original Indian settlements, Spanish occupation of area, American Revolution, the War of 1812, the Civil War, and occupation by U.S. forces during World War I.

Fort Morgan, near Gulf Shores, Ala., at the mouth of Mobile Bay, is called the Cradle of American History. It is said that Prince Madoc of Wales landed at this site in 1170—more than 300 years before Columbus set sail from Spain. Seven battles were fought here; seven flags have flown here. The fort played a major role in the Battle of Mobile Bay, and contains some of history's richest treasures.

Fort Morgan and the Fort Morgan Museum, Gulf Shores, Ala. The museum *(right center)* was completed in 1967. After Hurricane Frederic, September 1979, the museum was completely renovated and updated.

FORT CONDE MUSEUM

Royal St., Mobile, AL 36602
Telephone: (205) 438-7304
Director: Mrs. Eva Golson
Hours: Daily 9 A.M. to 5 P.M.
Cost of admission: Adults, $2; children, $1

Description: Located on Royal St. diagonally across from Mobile City Hall, the fort was headquarters for military rule of this coastal area by France, England, and Spain; home base at one time for the entire French Louisiana Territory; and protection against Indians and oftentimes hostile troops at Pensacola or New Orleans. The 1711 fort was of 14-inch cedar stakes that stood 13 feet high and was named Fort Louis de la Louisiane for King Louis XIV, who ordered the founding of Mobile. The name was changed in 1702 to Fort Conde in honor of a prominent French family. From 1724 to 1735, the French built a permanent brick and mortar fort within the temporary stockade. England acquired Fort Conde in 1763 at the end of the Seven Years War and renamed it Fort Charlotte in honor of the English king's wife. In 1780, Spain seized the city. They held it until 1813 when President James Madison ordered American troops to capture Mobile and end Spanish aid to the British.

Fort Conde, Mobile, Ala. Located directly on top of the I-10 tunnel in Mobile, this 18th-century French fort has been completely reconstructed to look as it did when it served as the first headquarters of the French empire in the new world.

EAGLE HISTORICAL SOCIETY MUSEUM

Eagle, AK 99738
Curator: Mrs. Elva Scott
Hours: June 1 through Labor Day
Cost of admission: Donations only

Description: Here are to be seen the remains of the U.S. Army post, Fort Egbert, which was maintained at Eagle during the years 1900–1911. It was from here that Billy Mitchell worked to complete the government telegraph line from Eagle to Valdez. Upon completion of the telegraph line Judge James Wickersham sent out the message that Roald Amundsen had discovered the long-sought Northwest Passage. At the far end of the old military parade ground (now used as an airstrip) sits the government Mule Barn. It remains the same minus the many patient animals whose names are still above the stalls. This is now the museum, where many military artifacts and tools are housed.

Eagle Historical Society Museum. Soldier undergoes glacier training on Eklunta Glacier, Alaska.

SITKA NATIONAL HISTORICAL PARK

P.O. Box 738
Sitka, AK 99835

Acting Superintendent: Gary J. Candelaria
Hours: Daily; closed Thanksgiving, Christmas, and New Year's Day
Cost of admission: Free to the public

Description: Sitka National Park is located in Alaska's southeastern panhandle, and is within easy walking distance of downtown Sitka. It was established in 1910 to commemorate the Battle of Sitka. This conflict arose when soldiers of the Russian army approached more than 700 Tlingit warriors, who were native to Alaska. The Tlingit and their families gathered in their large, palisaded fort. After a few skirmishes and a 6-day siege, the Tlingit ran out of ammunition and strategically withdrew. The Sitka Visitors Center holds numerous mementos of the battle and Russian occupation.

Exhibit on the Battle of Sitka, 1804, at the museum in Visitor Center, Sitka National Historical Park.

Visitor Center, Sitka National Historical Park.

This bronze placard on Castle Hill commemorates the transfer of Alaska from Russia to the U.S.

Russian graves adjacent to restored Russian blockhouse.

Nothing wrong with the photograph. The lettering on old locomotive is in reverse. Old wagon and ancient steamer are all part of Sitka National Park.

FORT BOWIE NATIONAL HISTORIC SITE

P.O. Box 158, Bowie, AZ 85605
Telephone: (602) 847-2500
Curator: Bill Hoy
Hours: Daily 8 A.M. to 5 P.M.
Cost of admission: Free to the public
Description: From the town of Willcox, located on I-10, drive 22 miles south on Ariz. 186 to the graded road leading east into Apache Pass; from the town of Bowie, also on I-10, drive south 12 miles on a graded dirt road that then bears west into Apache Pass. A park ranger is normally on duty at the museum to assist with historical interpretation. At Fort Bowie is the story of a determined Gen. George Crook struggling to cover a vast territory with a handful of men and an embittered Geronimo fighting against hopeless odds. Here is the drama of a band of Indians who tried to stop the soldiers of the U.S. Army—the vanguard of an alien civilization. Military and Indian warrior artifacts are to be seen in the museum.

Geronimo, leader of final renegade band, in Sierra Madre, Mexico. He surrendered four times, finally to Gen. Nelson A. Miles in 1886. Sent to Florida, Alabama, and finally to Fort Sill, Okla., Geronimo died in 1909.

Fort Bowie, Ariz. Zenith of Chiricachua Apache campaign in 1886.

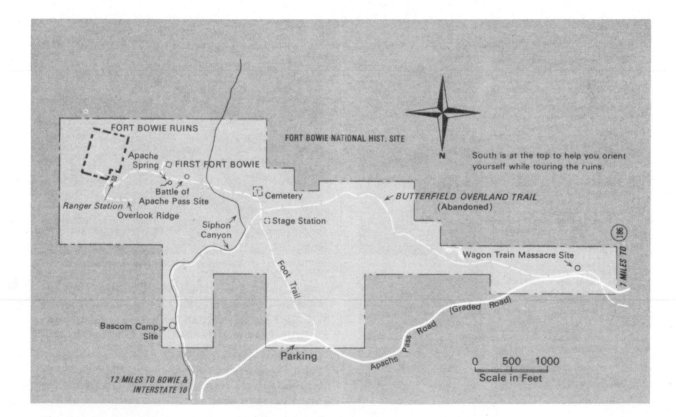

FORT VERDE STATE HISTORIC PARK

P.O. Box 397, Camp Verde, AZ 86322
Telephone: (602) 567-3275
Park Supervisor: Michael L. Sipes
Hours: Daily 8 A.M. to 5:30 P.M.; closed Christmas
Cost of admission: Adults (18 and over) 50¢
Description: The U.S. military occupation of Arizona's Verde Valley began in 1865. Soldiers were moved in at the request of settlers who had established farms near the Verde River–West Clear Creek Junction, 5 miles south of the present village of Camp Verde. Renamed Fort Verde in 1879, to signify the permanence of the garrison, the post was abandoned in 1891. The 10-acre state park now includes three original quarters, the administration (adjutant's) building, and a portion of the old parade ground. Today the Fort Verde Interpretative Center houses exhibits that include military accouterments, memorabilia, and displays pertaining to the Indian Wars.

The visitor center/museum at Fort Verde displays many Indian and military artifacts. It is the headquarters for a 10-acre site, which includes 3 original officers' quarters, the ruins of two others, the administration (adjutant's) building, and a portion of the old parade ground.

FORT APACHE

White Mountain Apache Culture Center, P. O. Box 507, Fort Apache, AZ 85926
Telephone: (602) 338-4625
Director: Edgar Perry
Hours: Monday through Friday 8 A.M. to 5 P.M.
Cost of admission: Donations only
Description: In 1969, the White Mountain Apache tribe established a culture center/museum at Fort Apache. It was dedicated to the preservation of the Apache language, culture, and history. The log cabin, built as commanding officer's quarters in 1871, at the west end of officers' row was chosen as the first headquarters for the new culture center/museum. The cabin was cleaned and repaired and a number of artifacts acquired and placed on display. A small library was established in one room of the cabin when the collection of Col. Harold B. Wharfield, commanding officer at Fort Apache in 1918, was donated to the Center. Apache craft work was gathered for display, and an oral history program was inaugurated, with more than 400 tapes accumulated and in the process of being transcribed. Uniforms, weapons, and other military artifacts have been added to the displays.

FORT HUACHUCA MUSEUM

P.O. Box 766, Fort Huachuca, AZ 85613
Telephone: (602) 538-5736
Museum Director: James P. Finley
Hours: Monday through Friday 9 A.M. to 4 P.M.;
weekends 1 P.M. to 4 P.M.; closed federal holidays
Cost of admission: Free to the public
Description: The historic Old Post is located at the mouth of Huachuca Canyon (southwest portion, Cochise County). It is just to the west of the Main Post with its modern structures and facilities. Unique in that almost all of its original 1890s buildings are still standing and in use, the Old Post retains much of its frontier atmosphere and the memories of its glorious past. Many people have passed this way, some to leave their mark for posterity, others to lapse into anonymity. Prehistoric man, early Indians, Spanish conquerors, Apaches, Mexicans, American settlers, soldiers, horse thieves, black men, yellow men, men of God, agents of the devil—they are what the Fort Huachuca Historical Museum is all about. Buildings abound with ancient uniforms, weapons, ammunition, saddlery, and the memorabilia of times when the U.S. Cavalry ruled the West.

The history of Fort Huachuca is presented live by skilled actors portraying frontier cavalrymen.

World War I is depicted to show the demise of the horse cavalry.

15

A representative of the White Mountain Apache Tribe presents the U.S. Army Indian Scout flag to the post commander, during ceremonies at the Sinew L. Riley Barracks dedication on January 25, 1974.

The late S. Sgt. Sinew L. Riley as a corporal near his wickiup home at Fort Huachuca, on his horse, Peanut. He was the highest ranking member of the last U.S. Army Indian Scout Detachment, which was deactivated at the fort in 1943.

ARIZONA NATIONAL GUARD HISTORICAL SOCIETY MUSEUM

5636 E. McDowell Rd., Phoenix, AZ 85008
Telephone: (602) 273-9700
Curator: Capt. George A. Crane
Hours: By appointment
Cost of admission: Museum not yet open to the public
Description: The museum houses militia artifacts from before the time Arizona became a state in 1912. Artifacts from the early days of Indian warfare, as well as times of settler troubles caused by the discovery of gold, silver, and copper, are on display. Military equipment from the various active service campaigns in which the Arizona National Guard served are shown, along with small arms, uniforms, field accouterments and devices from World War I and World War II.

Arizona National Guard Historical Society Museum. Prior to 1912 the regular army patroled the territory of Arizona. Here staff officers and their families are shown on one frontier post shortly after the Civil War.

FORT LOWELL MUSEUM

2900 N. Craycroft Rd., Tucson, AZ 85719
Telephone: (602) 885-3832
Curator: David T. Faust
Hours: Wednesday through Sunday 10 A.M. to 4 P.M.; closed legal holidays
Cost of admission: Free to the public
Description: The museum is furnished as it would have been in 1886 when inhabited by the post commander, Col. August V. Kautz, 8th U.S. Infantry, and his wife Fanny with their children. Rooms include a parlor, dining room, bedroom, and the commander's office. In the halls are a display case showing uniforms and equipment of the frontier soldier at Fort Lowell; and maps, photographs, and documents depicting interesting aspects of life at the post. A wall plaque gives the names and dates of all officers who commanded the post.

Fort Lowell Museum building contains room arrangements of the 1880s and showcases displaying uniforms and equipment of the frontier soldier.

PEA RIDGE NATIONAL MILITARY PARK

Pea Ridge, AR 72751

Hours: Daily 8 A.M. to 5 P.M.; extended hours during summer

Cost of admission: Free to the public

Description: Pea Ridge National Military Park is 10 miles northeast of Rogers, Ark. It commemorates the battle of Pea Ridge, March 1862, which saved Missouri for the Union, and is considered the strangest battle of the Civil War. Southern troops attacked from the north, while soldiers from Arkansas and Texas fought beside French-speaking Louisianans and Indian regiments serving under their own officers. Moreover, the Missouri State Guardsmen, who fought for the South, were not yet officially in the Confederate service. The Union soldiers came from Missouri, Iowa, Illinois, Indiana, and Ohio, and many spoke German as their first language. The visitor center houses a collection of displays, replicas, uniforms, weapons, and the scrub of battle.

The Elkhorn Tavern, located near Pea Ridge on the battlefield. Even in its closed, deserted state it is visited by scores daily.

FORT HUMBOLDT STATE HISTORIC PARK

3431 Fort Ave., Eureka, CA 95501
Telephone: (707) 443-7952
State Park Ranger I: Jacqueline A. Ball
Hours: Daily 8 A.M. to 5 P.M.; closed Christmas and New Year's Day
Cost of admission: Free to the public
Description: Fort Humboldt is a military fort that existed from 1853 to 1866 during the most intense period of settler/Indian conflict. It served as a supply base and prison camp. President Ulysses S. Grant was stationed at this fort early in his military career. Reconstruction of the fort is now underway with plans to restore all structures to their original appearance. The small Fort Humboldt room contains displays featuring military artifacts retrieved from the site, as well as old photographs of the fort.

The layout of Fort Humboldt greets the visitor.

Fort Humboldt. Historic hospital building, built in 1863.

19

FORT ROSS STATE HISTORIC PARK

19005 Coast Hwy. 1, Jenner, CA 95450
Telephone: (707) 847-3286
Superintendent: Ranger V. H. "Bud" Luckey
Hours: Daily 10 A.M. to 4:30 P.M.; closed
Thanksgiving, Christmas, and New Year's Day
Cost of admission: $2 per car; $8 per bus
Description: The original blockhouses and some parts of the stockade remained standing until the 1906 earthquake, and so it has been possible to reconstruct this 1812 fort with a high degree of accuracy. The 12-foot-high stockade, made entirely of hand-hewn redwood timbers and largely from original materials, includes three sally ports (large gateways with double doors hung on massive, hand-wrought iron hinges) that provided the only entrance to the stockade. Brass and iron cannons were placed in the blockhouses and also defended each sally port. Some descriptions say that the chapel also served as a bastion and that brass cannons were mounted on either side of the altar. Today, the seven-sided north blockhouse and the eight-sided south blockhouse are both open to the public and contain exhibits covering various aspects of the Fort Ross story.

Fort Ross chapel, built in 1825.

FORT TEJON STATE HISTORIC PARK

32251 Fort Tejon Rd., Lebec, CA 93206
Telephone: (805) 765-5004
Unit Ranger: Art Rüchter; Area Manager: K. R. Morgan
Hours: Daily 10 A.M. to 5 P.M.; closed
Thanksgiving, Christmas, and New Year's Day
Cost of admission: Adults (18 to 61 years) 50¢;
Children (6 to 17 years) 25¢; 62-plus years, 25¢

Description: Fort Tejon is one of California's outstanding historic parks. Located in Grapevine Canyon, Kern County, on Hwy. 99, and also I-5, it is 36 miles south of Bakersfield and 77 miles north of Los Angeles near the small community of Lebec. The present highway runs through the original area of the old fort. The old post is one of the significant remaining links to the early American occupation period. Established by the U.S. Army on August 10, 1854, Fort Tejon was abandoned 10 years later on September 11, 1864.

AMERICAN SOCIETY OF MILITARY HISTORY HERITAGE PARK AND MILITARY RESTORATION CENTER

1816 S. Figueroa St., Los Angeles, CA 90015
Telephone: (213) 746-1776
Director: Donald Michelson

Hours: Monday through Friday 9 A.M. to 5 P.M.;
weekends 10 A.M. to 3 P.M.
Cost of admission: Free to the public
Description: This is a 40-acre park dedicated to the American military heritage, said to contain the largest collection of military equipment in the West. Tanks, trucks, guns, artifacts, and flags are on display. The submarine USSN *Roncador*, a World War II fleet-type submarine is on exhibit and open for tours.

PRESIDIO OF MONTEREY (Army) MUSEUM

Bldg. 113, Presidio of Monterey, Monterey, CA 93940
Telephone: (408) 242-8414
Curator: Margaret B. Admas
Hours: Thursday through Monday 8:30 A.M. to 12:30 P.M., 1:30 P.M. to 4 P.M.; closed Thursdays following Monday federal holidays.
Cost of admission: Free to the public
Description: The Presidio of Monterey Museum sits on a strategic and historic hill overlooking the Monterey Bay. There are several points of interest within easy walking distance of the parking areas in front of the museum building. From the time of its original corrugated-iron construction in 1909, the museum building has been continuously used for a variety of purposes: warehouse, magazine, medical center, tack/supply room, Boy Scout hall, and youth center. In 1965 it was selected for conversion to an army museum, and it was opened to the public on April 20, 1968. The facade designed by local artist Bruce Ariss resembles an adobe structure of the Mexican Era.

The museum traces the history of Presidio ("Old Fort") Hill from the Rumsen Indian occupation to the present. Its collection includes Spanish, Mexican, and early American artifacts; dioramas of early forts on the hill, Gold Rush era in California, Buffalo Soldiers of the 9th Cavalry; Philippine insurrection, World War I, and World War II. Currently, the Presidio also houses the Defense Language School, largest language-teaching facility in the Free World.

One of the many dioramas depicting the evolution of the Presidio of Monterey.

The museum at the Presidio of Monterey.

FORT POINT NATIONAL HISTORIC SITE

P.O. Box 29333, Presidio of San Francisco, CA 94129

Telephone: (415) 556-1693

Site Manager: Charles S. Hawkins

Hours: Daily 10 A.M. to 5 P.M.

Cost of admission: Free to the public

Description: Fort Point is a national historic site with exhibits and displays of military equipment and artillery (muzzle-loading) weapons.

Fort Point and the Golden Gate Bridge, looking north toward Marin County.

PRESIDIO ARMY MUSEUM

Bldg. 2, Presidio of San Francisco, CA 94129

Telephone: (415) 561-3319

Director: John P. Lanellier; Curator: Eric A. Saul

Hours: Tuesday through Sunday 10 A.M. to 4 P.M.

Cost of admission: Free to the public

Description: In 1776 Spain's military forces arrived in the Bay Area as both soldiers and settlers. In 1822 the flag of Mexico replaced Spain's ensign. The Mexican garrison remained in control until 1846, when the Stars and Stripes first flew over San Francisco. The Presidio Army Museum shows early U.S. uniforms and equipage. It also has displays on the Spanish occupation of the area from 1776 through 1826. Dioramas include the Presidio of 1806, the earthquake and fire of 1906, the Pan-Pacific International Exposition of 1915, and a World War I trench scene. The museum also has a "rotational" gallery, changing shows every 6 months.

A 10-inch Rodman cannon being repositioned within the old garrison at the San Francisco Presidio.

The Presidio Army Museum underwent a complete renovation and modernization during the years 1979–1980. Special exhibits now feature the influence of minorities on California history.

ANGEL ISLAND STATE PARK

P.O. Box 318, Tiburon, CA 94920
Telephone: (415) 435-1915
Supervising Ranger: Michael B. Garguilo
Hours: Daily 8 A.M. to sunset
Cost of admission: Free to the public.
Description: Buildings comprising Camp Rey-nolds (1863–1900) and Fort McDowell (1900–1946) and their gun batteries can be viewed by walking around the island. A visitor center contains exhibits, maps, and artifacts. It is located at park headquarters, where ferryboats land.

U.S. 32-pounder on barbette carriage (1860), Angel Island State Park.

DRUM BARRACKS— CIVIL WAR MUSEUM

1055 Cary Ave., Wilmington, CA 90744
Telephone: (213) 834-1078
President: Mrs. Joan Lorenzen
Hours: By appointment
Cost of admission: Adults (18 and over) $1; 12 to 17 years 50¢; 2 to 11 years 25¢; under 2 free
Description: On display are Civil War memorabilia—uniforms, guns, rifles, pictures, Gatling guns, cannon, saddles, furniture, pianos, miniature structural display of Camp Drum and of Drum Barracks—an orientation room containing founding society members' photos and histories, framed resolutions, and plaques awarded the society for the preservation of Drum Barracks, postcards and square nails exchanged by donations. Outside may be seen a rose bush planted in 1874, historical site plaques, a brick patio made from the brick fireplaces which are now restored as modern artificial ones.

Drum Barracks, Civil War Museum, Wilmington, Calif.

FORT CARSON MUSEUM OF THE ARMY IN THE WEST

Fort Carson, CO 80913
Telephone: (303) 579-2908
Curator: James J. Busch
Hours: Monday through Friday 9 A.M. to 5 P.M.; closed Saturday, Sunday, and all federal holidays
Cost of admission: Free to the public
Description: Fort Carson is 1 mile south of Colorado Springs. The museum displays military artifacts and memorabilia acquired primarily from veterans of units that have trained or passed through Fort Carson. The collection includes weapons, uniforms, and equipment from 1775 to the present. There is an extensive display of distinctive unit insignia and a large collection of military headgear. Exhibits also tell the story of the 4th Infantry Division (Mechanized), currently stationed at Fort Carson.

Weapons at the Fort Carson museum range in age from the Civil War, through the Franco-Prussian War, to both World Wars.

MEMORIAL MILITARY MUSEUM, INC.

61 Center St., Bristol, CT 06010

Telephone: (203) 583-5466

Curator: John J. Denehy, Jr.

Hours: April through October, Friday 7 P.M. to 9 P.M.; Veteran's Day, November 11, 1 P.M. to 4 P.M.; weekdays 9 A.M. to 4 P.M. by appointment

Cost of admission: Free to the public

Description: This museum is located in a working National Guard Armory. It contains photos, uniforms, medals, small arms, edged weapons, and war souvenirs obtained by Bristol area veterans which have been donated or loaned for display. All branches of the uniformed services are represented, from the time of the Civil War to the present. Displays of special significance are: Confederate flag captured during Battle of New Bern, N.C., in 1862; a gong alarm from the battleship USS *Maine;* relics from Japanese aircraft downed during raid on Pearl Harbor; autographs of Nazi war criminals; and numerous relics from World War II combat areas.

The Pacific Theatre of World War II has numerous special displays.

Uniforms, guidons, and captured flags are on display at the Memorial Military Museum, Bristol, Conn.

76TH INFANTRY DIVISION MUSEUM FOUNDATION

700 S. Quaker Lane, West Hartford, CT 06110
Telephone: (203) 236-2820
Director: Maj. Lawrence P. Lindquest
Hours: Monday through Friday 8 A.M. to 4 P.M.
Cost of admission: Free to the public
Description: The museum houses World War I and World War II Allied and German military items, including heraldry and regalia of battle. Helmets, medals, insignia, uniforms, markings, news items, badges, and photographs are on display.

The 76th Infantry Division Museum has a large collection of both enemy and friendly force uniforms, caps, medals, badges, guns, and ammunition.

FORT DELAWARE

Pea Patch Island, Delaware City, DE 19706
Cost of admission: Boat fare—adults $2.25; children $1.25
Description: Boats leave Delaware City at regular intervals starting at 11 A.M. Last return boat leaves the fort at 6 P.M. The pentagon-shaped fort covers about 6 of the 70 acres that are considered fast land. It has a parade ground within its walls that spanned more than 2 acres. It was reduced in size in 1898 when emplacements for three 12-inch disappearing guns were built in the southern half of the enclosure.

Fort Delaware, located on a remote island, is surrounded by a deep moat.

Fort Delaware was used as a prison for Confederate soldiers, both able-bodied and recovering wounded.

ARMED FORCES MEDICAL MUSEUM

Bldg. 54, Command Forces Institute of Pathology, 6825 16th St. NW, Washington, DC 20306
Telephone: (202) 576-2418
Associate Director: Edward R. White, M.D., J.D.
Hours: Daily noon to 6 P.M.; closed Thanksgiving, Christmas, New Year's Day
Cost of admission: Free to the public
Description: In 1812 there was growing concern over the loss of life and limbs from wounds encountered on the battlefield, thus the Army Medical Museum was founded as a means of preserving and studying casualties. Today the Medical Museum contains specimens representing nearly every disease afflicting man, as well as extensive collections of medical, surgical, and diagnostic instruments and related medical items. Many of these items are not on exhibit at any one time, but they can be made available on request to anyone who is engaged in serious study and research.

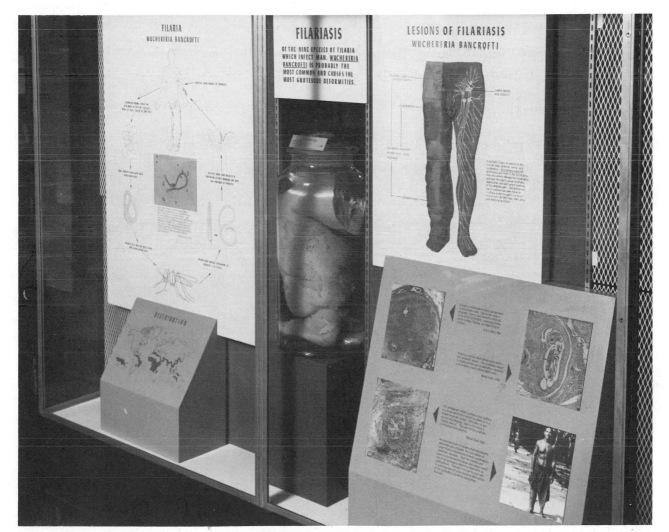

Armed Forces Medical Museum. The causes, history, and, to some extent, the cures of diseases are depicted through graphs, charts, and cut-away displays.

DAR MUSEUM

1776 D Street NW, Washington, DC 20006
Telephone: (202) 628-1776
Curator: Mrs. Jean Taylor Federico
Hours: Monday through Friday 8:30 A.M. to 4 P.M.
Cost of admission: Free to the public
Description: The museum offers a small collection of military uniforms, Revolutionary weapons and artifacts of the battlefield.

The front of the DAR Building, which houses the DAR Museum.

NATIONAL GUARD HERITAGE GALLERY

1 Massachusetts Ave. NW, Washington, DC 20001
Telephone: (202) 789-0031
Assistant Curator: Col. Leslie H. Cross, USA (Ret.)
Hours: Daily 9 A.M. to 4 P.M.
Cost of admission: Free to the public
Description: The gallery, located on the main floor of the National Guard Memorial Building, is but 1 block from the National Visitor's Center and Union Station. It can be reached from locations in the District of Columbia, Maryland, and Virginia by Metro (subway) or by bus. Although modest in size compared to many better known institutions in a city of museums and monuments, it has been characterized by one art critic as "a small gem of a museum." Its collection of Militia and National Guard artifacts, dioramas, prints, and audiovisual displays provide a unique and educational view of American history.

National Guard Heritage Gallery. Three-dimensional display of young George Washington as a Virginia militiaman.

Panorama showing the hell of moving cannons at Valley Forge.

NATIONAL RIFLE ASSOCIATION FIREARMS MUSEUM

1600 Rhode Island Ave. NW, Washington, DC 20036

Telephone: (202) 828-6194

Curator: Dan R. Abbey, Jr.

Hours: Daily 10 A.M. to 4 P.M.; closed Thanksgiving, Christmas, New Year's Day, and Easter

Cost of admission: Free to the public

Description: One of the largest concentrated displays of guns in the United States, the museum contains more than 1,200 rifles, carbines, shotguns, airguns, and pistols. Basic models and types are well represented, along with many rare variations. There are exhibits of sporting arms, military weapons (no full automatics), and police handguns.

Famous guns and famous owners.

National Rifle Association Firearms Museum. The Ruger .44 handgun, one of the most popular in the Old West.

PENTAGON

Washington, DC 20301
Telephone: (202) 695-1776
In Charge of Tours: Address queries to OASD-PA-Pentagon Tours
Hours: Daily 9 A.M. to 3:30 P.M.
Cost of admission: Free to the public
Description: A guided tour of the halls of the Pentagon (apply at tour desk) is a must for every student of military history. Its collections include original combat art galore, montages of all past presidents, POW (prisoner of war) paintings and artifacts, a great array of military photographs taken in combat, models of combat equipment, a large collection of flags, recruitment posters from all wars, a Marine Corps alcove, a Navy corridor, an Army corridor, and an Air Force corridor. Each corridor is replete with models, oil paintings, photographs, and artifacts. There is also a correspondents' corridor; a *Time-Life* corridor; and, above all, a Hall of Heroes, featuring a shrine to Medal-of-Honor winners.

The Hall of Heroes.

All tours in the Pentagon are guided tours. Here a uniformed Army spokesman tells of the winners of the Medal of Honor, America's highest award for valor.

A case dedicated to Richard Tregaskis, war correspondent.

FORT CLINCH STATE PARK

2601 Atlantic Ave., Fernandina Beach, FL 32034
Telephone: (904) 261-4212
Superintendent: Capt. Roy Kemp
Hours: Daily 8 A.M. to 5 P.M.
Cost of admission: 25¢

Description: The entire fort, part of the Totter System of Coastal Fortifications, is in excellent state of preservation. On display are kitchens, quartermaster building, jail, officers' quarters, carpenter's shop, bakeries, blacksmith shop, infirmary, ordnance room, guard room, five bastions, eight 10-inch guns, ramparts, parade grounds, and sally ports. A newly opened display museum shows many military artifacts.

FORT JEFFERSON NATIONAL MONUMENT, FLORIDA

Address inquiries to: Superintendent, Everglades
Nat'l Park, P.O. Box 279, Homestead, FL 33030
Cost of admission: Free to the public

Description: Fort Jefferson, largest of the 19th-century American coastal forts, is the central feature of the seven Dry Tortugas islands and the surrounding shoals and waters of the Gulf of Mexico that make up Fort Jefferson National Monument. Though off the beaten path, the island and its fort offer a good deal for sightseers. Transportation is available from Key West by boat and amphibious aircraft. Information on these charter boats and flights can be obtained from the Key West Chamber of Commerce. For almost 10 years after the Civil War, Fort Jefferson remained a prison. Among the prisoners sent there in 1865 were several of the "Lincoln conspirators," among them Dr. Samuel A. Mudd, who, knowing nothing of President Lincoln's assassination, had set the broken leg of the fugitive killer, John Wilkes Booth.

Aerial view of Fort Jefferson. Almost 70 miles west of Key West, Fla., is a cluster of coral keys called Dry Tortugas. In 1513, Spanish explorer Ponce de Leon named them as *las Tortugas* (the Turtles), because of "the great amount of turtles that there do breed." The later name, Dry Tortugas, warns mariners that there is no fresh water here.

Coast Guardsmen from a nearby station listen with avid interest while a National Park ranger relates the picturesque history of Fort Jefferson over a 10-inch coast artillery cannon.

FORT CAROLINE NATIONAL MEMORIAL

12713 Caroline Rd., Jacksonville, FL 32225
Telephone: (904) 641-7155
Superintendent: Charles L. Vial
Hours: Daily 9 A.M. to 5 P.M.; closed Christmas and New Year's Day
Cost of admission: Free to the public
Description: The memorial is about 10 miles east of Jacksonville and 5 miles west of Mayport. It can be reached by Fla. 10; turn off on the St. John's Bluff Rd. or Monument Rd., then proceed east on Fort Caroline Rd. The monument houses period pieces from when Europeans attempted to settle in the New World—armor, navigational instruments, documents, and the

Fort Caroline National Memorial. Visitor center.

33

Field guns are properly positioned and stand guard.

works of several famous artists. There are a number of displays showing Timucua Indian artifacts and a dugout canoe. There is a Renaissance room, with oak paneling from a 16th-century room and, in the interior of the chamber, a 16th-century spinet. Fort Caroline marks the site of the first military confrontation between France and Spain for supremacy over a region that is now part of the U.S.

LIGHTHOUSE MILITARY MUSEUM

Whitehead St. at Truman Ave., Key West, FL 33040

Telephone: (305) 294-0012

Cost of admission: Adults $1.75; children 50¢; active duty military and families free

Description: The lighthouse and lighthouse keeper's home were built in 1846. Historical military memorabilia; photos; and U.S. Navy, Army, Marines, Air Force, Coast Guard, and NASA displays may be viewed. Records and photos of presidential visits to Key West from Grant's in 1867 to Kennedy's in 1961 are on display, with an emphasis on Truman, who often vacationed in Key West. Exhibits include a presidential flag presented to the officers and men of the Marine Corps stationed in the Key West area; a submarine periscope; a historical bell from the ill-fated submarine S-51; artifacts of the first chaplain at the South Pole, a member of Operation Deepfreeze; a model of a seaplane tender; a 2-man Japanese submarine captured at Pearl Harbor, from which the first prisoner of war was taken December 8, 1941; a TF-9 Cougar plane flown by the Navy's famous Blue Angels; a 2.75-inch Mighty Mouse rocket; and numerous displays.

The Key West Lighthouse built in 1846, and Japanese 2-man submarine captured at Pearl Harbor.

OLUSTEE BATTLEFIELD STATE HISTORIC SITE

P.O. Box 40, Olustee, FL 32072
Telephone: (904) 752-3866
Superintendent: T. E. Cravey
Hours: Daily 9 A.M. to 5 P.M.
Cost of admission: Free to the public
Description: **This memorial to the major engagement of the Civil War in Florida, Olustee Battlefield, covers 270 acres on U.S. 90 2 miles east of Olustee. The campaign that culminated in the Battle of Olustee began when General Q. A. Gillmore sent a Federal expedition from Hilton Head, S.C., to occupy Jacksonville for a fourth time. The general objectives were to break up communications between east and west Florida, thus depriving the Confederacy of food supplies drawn from the east and central Florida; to procure for Northern use Florida cotton, turpentine, and timber; to obtain recruits for Negro regiments; and to induce Unionists in east Florida to organize a loyal state government. The museum offers exhibits that interpret the Confederate victory in this conflict.**

Olustee Battlefield. The museum offers exhibits that interpret this Confederate victory. The battlefield itself is well marked by a trail and signs along the battle lines.

HERE WAS FOUGHT ON FEBRUARY 20, 1864
THE BATTLE OF OCEAN POND
UNDER THE IMMEDIATE COMMAND OF
GENERAL ALFRED HOLT COLQUITT
"HERO OF OLUSTEE"

THIS DECISIVE ENGAGEMENT PREVENTED A
SHERMAN-LIKE INVASION OF GEORGIA FROM
THE SOUTH.

ERECTED APRIL 20, 1936
BY THE ALFRED HOLT COLQUITT CHAPTER
UNITED DAUGHTERS OF THE CONFEDERACY
GA. DIV.

A monument that speaks for itself at Olustee Battlefield Site, Fla.

FORT REDOUBT

Pensacola Naval Air Station, Pensacola, FL 32508
Address inquiries to: National Park Service, P.O.
Box 100, Gulf Breeze, FL 32561
Cost of admission: Free to the public
Description: On the mainland bluff, inside Pensacola Naval Air Station, are a number of historic fortifications, among them Fort Redoubt. These forts were built to defend the channel entrance to the harbor. The interiors of these forts, and their many artifacts, are closed temporarily. They can only be visited by special permission.

These 24-pound siege guns are cradled on the parade ground within the walls of Fort Redoubt, Pensacola Naval Air Station.

CASTILLO DE SAN MARCOS NATIONAL MONUMENT

1 Castillo Dr., St. Augustine, FL 32084
Telephone: (904) 829-6506
Acting Superintendent: Robert C. Amdor
Hours: Daily, winter 8:30 A.M. to 5:15 P.M.;
summer 9 A.M. to 5:45 P.M.; closed Christmas
Cost of admission: Free to the public
Description: The fort is located in what is now part of downtown St. Augustine. It is the oldest masonry fortification within the continental United States and a symbol of Spain's early colonization of Florida. It was set aside for preservation in 1924 and included as a historical area of the National Park System in 1935. Grim, vital, defiant of time, this monument of Spain's hours of greatness seems still to be peering defensively out upon the Gulf Stream, seems still to be guarding the homecoming galleons from the corsair. To touch its gray outer walls, to wander among its rooms, to climb its ramp and look out upon the blue waters of Matanzas Bay is to wish to know the story of Spain in America; and here a part of it is beautifully told as in no other military museum in the world.

Where a drawbridge once stood, this sturdy structure admits thousands of visitors. In 1672 ground was first broken for this fortress, which was completed in 1695. In later years it was enlarged.

From the air, Castillo de San Marcos reveals its true beauty. The entrance, seen to the left of the castle, was once an outer guardhouse leading to a drawbridge over a moat.

FORT MATANZAS NATIONAL MONUMENT

1 Castillo Dr., St. Augustine, FL 32084
Telephone: (904) 829-6506
Acting Superintendent: Robert C. Amdor
Hours: Daily, winter 8:30 A.M. to 5:15 P.M.;
summer 9 A.M. to 5:45 P.M.; closed Christmas
Cost of admission: Free to the public

Description: The park is 14 miles south of St. Augustine and can be reached via Fla. A1A on Anastasia Island. A free ferryboat operates between Anastasia Island and Rattlesnake Island (site of the fort). Check with ranger in charge at the site for ferryboat schedule; telephone (904) 471-0116. Slaughters is the English translation for Matanzas. Here, on September 29 and October 12, 1565, between 200 and 300 Frenchmen, all Huguenots, were put to the sword by the Spaniards. These Frenchmen were less than half the force that had set out from Fort Caroline to attack Menendez at St. Augustine. Their ships had been scattered and wrecked by a hurricane. President Calvin Coolidge set aside Fort Matanzas and certain surrounding lands, by proclamation in 1924, to be preserved as a site of historic significance.

Fort Matanzas, on one of the Gulf Islands, is fairly steeped in history. In 1569 a wooden watchtower and a thatched hut were built at Matanzas Inlet to house 6 soldiers who took turns scanning the horizon for pirates or enemy ships. If a sail was sighted, a man in a log canoe set out to warn St. Augustine. From that humble housing chore it grew into a sizable armed fort.

STATE ARSENAL

St. Augustine, FL 32984
Telephone: (904) 824-8461
Director: Col. Frank Persons
Hours: By appointment
Cost of admission: Free to all military and others by special arrangement

Description: The State Arsenal, one of several buildings comprising St. Francis Barracks, is one of the oldest buildings in St. Augustine. It is now headquarters for the Military Department, State of Florida, and the Florida National Guard. This structure has not always been a military headquarters; it was originally a Spanish Franciscan monastery and convent. This reservation, comprising the barracks lot, the military hospital lot, the powder house lot, and the "Hedrick lot" or powder magazine lot, contained about 20 acres. In 1907 it was leased and later conveyed to the state of Florida for military use. Today, it is a 4.2-acre reservation containing the headquarters for the National Guard, the residence of the Adjutant General and members of his staff, plus a collection of memorabilia.

State Arsenal. Name and sign on door.

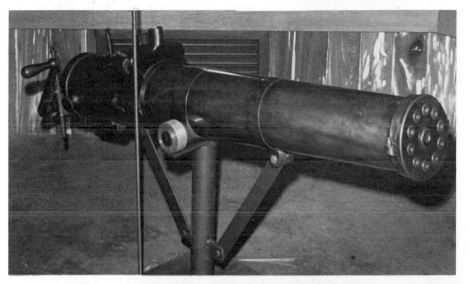

MUSEUM
FLORIDA NATIONAL GUARD
AND MILITIA

DEDICATED TO THE OFFICERS
AND MEN OF THE FLORIDA NATIONAL
GUARD AND MILITIA

Navy Gatling gun and display of current and recent equipment.

Flag room with retired unit colors.

FORT PICKENS

Santa Rosa Island, at entrance to Pensacola Bay, FL

Address inquiries to: National Park Service, P.O. Box 100, Gulf Breeze, FL 32561

Cost of admission: Free to the public

Description: Massive, 5-sided Fort Pickens on Santa Rosa Island was built (1829–34) soon after Florida was ceded to the United States by Spain in 1821. The fort protected an important naval shipyard on Pensacola Bay. Fort Pickens came under fire only once, when Confederates tried without success to capture it early in the Civil War. Later the fort was used as a military prison. Geronimo, leader of the Chiricahua Apaches, was kept prisoner here. Long-range coastal guns were mounted during the Spanish-American War, and the ordnance was modernized again during World War I and World War II when artillery and antiaircraft units trained on the island. Today Battery Cooper and Battery 234 with guns mounted represent this last period of seacoast defenses.

An ancient 10-inch coast artillery gun makes a fine place for boys to climb, play, and use their imaginations. At their feet can be seen the great breadth of the Gulf of Mexico.

The massive, 5-sided Fort Pickens was built in 1820–34. Soon after construction began, Florida was ceded to the U.S. by Spain. The fort was in use through the end of World War II. It is now part of the Gulf Islands, Fla.-Mississippi National Park.

ANDERSONVILLE NATIONAL HISTORIC SITE

Georgia Hwy. 49, Andersonville, GA 31711
Telephone: (912) 924-0343
Hours: Daily; closed Christmas
Cost of admission: Free to the public
Description: Andersonville National Historic Site is 9 miles northeast of Americus on Ga. 49. The 470-acre park, consisting of the national cemetery and the prison site, exemplifies the grim life suffered by prisoners—North and South—during the Civil War. The first Union prisoners were brought to Andersonville in February 1864. Approximately 400 more arrived each day during the next few months, and by the end of July some 31,678 men were confined in a prison originally built for 10,000. The largest number held at any one time was more than 32,000. In August 1864, handicapped by deteriorating economic conditions, an inadequate transportation system, and the necessity of concentrating all available resources on the army, the Confederate government was unable to provide adequate housing, food, clothing, and medical care to the federal captives. These conditions, along with a breakdown of the prisoner exchange system, created much suffering and a high mortality rate.

Providence Spring located in prison site area at Andersonville.

New York monument located in the national cemetery at Andersonville.

Memorial containing lines from Lincoln's Gettysburg Address.

ATLANTA HISTORICAL SOCIETY

3099 Andrews Dr. NW, Atlanta, GA 30355
Telephone: (404) 261-1837
Curator: Ms. Lisa Reynolds
Hours: Tuesday through Saturday 10:30 A.M. to
4:30 P.M. Tours every half hour beginning at
10:30. Last tour at 4 P.M. Sunday, 2 P.M. to 4:30
P.M. Closed Christmas Eve, Christmas, and New
Year's Day.
Cost of admission: Free, house tours $1 each
Description: Swan House is an 1828 Palladian-style mansion which has been authentically furnished with many 18th-century English pieces. Tullie Smith House is an 1840 plantation-plains–style farmhouse with authentic outbuildings and furnishings.

Portrait of Gen. Joseph E. Johnston, CSA, Swan House.

Swan House, Atlanta Historical Society.

GEORGIA VETERAN MEMORIAL STATE PARK

Rt. 3, Cordele, GA 31015
Telephone: (912) 273-2190
Hours: Daily 8 A.M. to 5 P.M.; closed Thanksgiving, Christmas, and New Year's Day

Cost of admission: Free to the public
Description: On display are relics of past military, documents, uniforms, artifacts, and items used in several wars—rifles, knives, bayonets, Civil War minié balls, swords, bazookas, hand grenades, plus other pieces of military equipment. Each item's use is briefly explained, and all branches of the service are represented.

FORT KING GEORGE HISTORIC SITE

P.O. Box 711, Darien, GA 31305
Telephone: (912) 437-4770
Superintendent: Norman Edwards
Hours: Tuesday through Saturday 9 A.M. to 5 P.M.; Sunday 2 P.M. to 5:30 P.M.; closed Mondays, except state holidays
Cost of admission: Free to the public
Description: Fort King George is located on the outskirts of Darien, east of U.S. 17. Its collections range from the oldest to most recent specimens of coastal Georgia's history. Once the site of a large Indian village and Spanish mission, Fort King George was built by the British to block French colonization of the Altamaha River and coastal Georgia. The British and their Indian allies had driven the Guale Indians and Spanish from the coast by 1702. The museum interprets the Guale Indians, Spanish mission era, European rivalry for the Southeast which culminated in Fort King George, the Scots colony of Darien, and the timber industry.

Visitor Center/Museum, Fort King George.

NATIONAL INFANTRY MUSEUM

Bldg. 396, Fort Benning, GA 31905
Telephone: (404) 545-2958 or 544-4762
Curator: Lt. Col. Dick D. Grube, RA (Ret.)
Hours: Tuesday through Friday 10 A.M. to 4:30
P.M.; weekends 12:30 P.M. to 4:30 P.M.; closed
Thanksgiving, Christmas, and New Year's Day
Cost of admission: Free to the public
Description: Fort Benning is 5 miles south of

Columbus. The museum collection consists of military equipment, weapons, uniforms from the U.S. and many foreign nations, but it includes much more than military hardware. Fine examples of military art and sculpture by noted artists are also on display, along with documents by more than half of the Presidents of the U.S., and one of the most complete collections of small arms in the country. In front of the museum is an exhibit of artillery pieces and armored vehicles.

The National Infantry Museum, Bldg. 396, Fort Benning, Ga.

Spanish-American War uniform.

World War II display area.

49

U.S. ARMY SIGNAL MUSEUM

Fort Gordon, GA 30905
Telephone: (404) 791-2818
Hours: Monday through Friday 8 A.M. to 4:30
P.M.; weekends noon to 4:30 P.M.; closed holidays
Cost of admission: Free to the public

Description: Fort Gordon is 5 miles southwest of Augusta. From I-20, near Augusta, turn onto Bobby Jones Exp. east; go 3 miles to Fort Gordon turnoff (Rt. 78). Take turnoff 3 miles to main gate, Fort Gordon. Location of U.S. Army Signal Museum is Commandant Rd. and 38th St., 5 miles from main gate. Museum houses personal items of Brig. Gen. Albert J. Myer, founder of the Signal Corps, and signal artifacts from World War I through World War II. A new Signal Corps Museum, with over 50,000 square feet of usable space, is being constructed on a wooded hill near the Dwight D. Eisenhower Army Medical Center. The new building will incorporate technological developments in communications, computers, television, photography, cryptology, and meteorology.

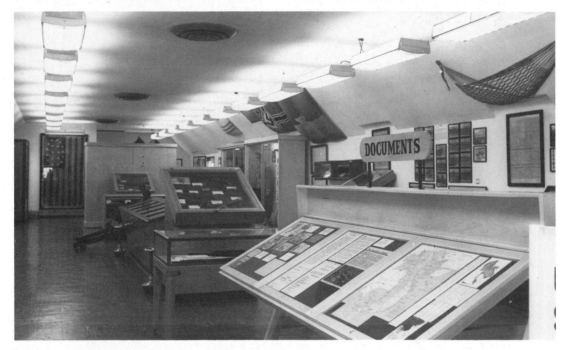

Displays at U.S. Army Signal Museum, Fort Gordon, Ga.

CHICKAMAUGA-CHATTANOOGA NATIONAL MILITARY PARK

P.O. Box 2126, Fort Oglethorpe, GA 30742
Telephone: (404) 866-9241
Superintendent: M. Ann Belkov
Hours: Daily 8 A.M. to 4:45 P.M.
Cost of admission: Free to the public

Description: Chickamauga-Chattanooga National Military Park, created by an act of Congress on August 9, 1890, is the oldest and largest National Military Park. Visitor center and museum is on U.S. 27, south of Fort Oglethorpe. Containing over 8,000 acres, the park is made up of several units, the largest of which is Chickamauga Battlefield, about 10 miles south of Chattanooga. Other areas include portions of Lookout Mountain, Missionary Ridge, and Orchard Knob, all scenes of major fighting in the Battle of Chattanooga. Visitor center includes 20-minute slide presentation, exhibits, and the Fuller Gun Collection, containing 355 American shoulder arms. Seven-mile self-guided tour covers battlefield. Additional exhibits in the Ochs Museum on Lookout Mountain.

View from Lookout Mountain, Chattanooga National Military Park.

Fuller Gun Collection.

THE
CLAUD E. AND ZENADA O. FULLER
COLLECTION OF
AMERICAN MILITARY FIREARMS
DONATED TO
THE PEOPLE OF THE UNITED STATES

This collection contains samples of
almost every type of long arm used by
the military forces of America

24TH INFANTRY DIVISION AND FORT STEWART MUSEUM

Address inquiries to: AFZP-DPT-P, Fort Stewart, GA 31314

Telephone: (912) 767-4891

Curator: Dr. Ray J. Kinder

Hours: Monday through Friday 1 P.M. to 5 P.M.; weekends 2 P.M. to 6 P.M.; closed federal holidays

Cost of admission: Free to the public

Description: On display are arms, equipment, uniforms, insignia, decorations, awards, documents, and pictures relating to all U.S. wars from the Civil War through the Vietnam War, especially as related to divisional units. The museum park includes tanks, towed and self-propelled artillery pieces and mounts, half-tracks, a Korean-War ambulance and Jeep, and a World War II antiaircraft searchlight; there is also a Korean-War helicopter (OH-13). An exhibit portrays the division's tour in Germany (1958–68), which includes NATO and Warsaw Pact uniforms, arms, equipment, insignia, and awards. Throughout Fort Stewart's history there have been bred famous units, such as Merrill's Marauders; each is highlighted by a special exhibit.

Banners commemorate the wars against the Plains Indians.

Armored vehicles flank entrance to 24th Infantry Division and Fort Stewart Museum.

World War I display.

KENNESAW MOUNTAIN NATIONAL BATTLEFIELD PARK

P.O. Box 1167, Marietta, GA 30061

Telephone: (404) 427-4686

Curator: D. A. Brown

Hours: Daily 8:30 A.M. to 5 P.M.

Cost of admission: Free to the public

Description: Kennesaw Mountain National Battlefield Park is located 2 miles north of Marietta, Georgia, a short distance off U.S. 41. At the visitor center, museum exhibits and a 15-minute slide program depict the history of the Atlanta Campaign during the Civil War, with emphasis on fighting around Kennesaw Mountain. In the series of military events that led to the fall of Atlanta in the third year of the Civil War, the battle of Kennesaw Mountain was decisive. Here Confederate soldiers bested their Northern opponents on the battlefield but had to give up their positions when the larger Union army succeeded in moving around the mountain toward its objective. The siege and fall of Atlanta soon followed. Then Sherman began his devastating march to the sea. Uniforms, weapons, equipment, and military accouterments are featured.

Illinois State Memorial, Kennesaw Mountain National Battlefield Park.

Visitor center/museum at Kennesaw Mountain National Battlefield Park.

SUNBURY HISTORIC SITE

Rt. 1, P.O. Box 236, Midway, GA 31320
Telephone: (912) 884-5999
Director: Joe H. Thompson
Hours: Monday through Saturday 9 A.M. to 5 P.M.;
Sunday 2 P.M. to 5:30 P.M.; closed Thanksgiving
and Christmas

Cost of admission: Free to the public
Description: Located on the site is an 1814 earthen fortification, Fort Defiance, which was built on the location of a Revolutionary War fort named Fort Morris. The museum contains exhibits and artifacts of all three fortifications, and the town itself, from 1758 through the Civil War. There is also a slide show on the Revolutionary War in Georgia.

FORT MCALLISTER HISTORIC SITE

P.O. Box 198, Richmond Hill, GA 31324
Telephone: (912) 727-2339
Curator: Roger S. Durham
Hours: Tuesday through Saturday 9 A.M. to 5 P.M.;
Sunday 2 P.M. to 5:30 P.M.; closed Thanksgiving
and Christmas
Cost of admission: Free to the public
Description: Fort McAllister is 25 miles south of Savannah and can be reached via Ga. 144 from both I-95 and U.S. 17. The site adjoins Richmond Hill State Park, where camping and picnicking are available. The fall of Fort McAllister marked the end of Sherman's March to the Sea. Communications were opened via the Ogeechee between the Union army and the fleet. The loss of the Confederate works rendered the further defense of Savannah useless. Seven days later the city was evacuated by Gen. William J. Hardee, CSA. The museum, which holds many Confederate and Union mementos, also contains an impressive record of the Confederate blockade-runner *Nashville*. The building for the museum was completed in 1963, 100 years after the great bombardments by Union ironclads.

Bunkers, trenches, revetments, and palisades have all been restored.

FORT FREDERICA NATIONAL MONUMENT VISITOR CENTER

Rt. 4, Box 286-C, St. Simons Island, GA 31522
Telephone: (912) 638-3639
Hours: Daily 9 A.M. to 5 P.M.
Cost of admission: Free to the public

Description: Banners describe the important events relating to the fort and to the town of Frederica. Numerous military artifacts are displayed; these have been excavated from the various house lots in the historic town. A 3-dimensional model of the town and fort offers visitors some idea of how historians feel the area appeared during its heyday in the mid-1740s. Bloody Marsh Battle Site, 6 miles south of Frederica, commemorates the engagement that proved to be the turning point in the Spanish invasion of Georgia. There, on July 7, 1742, an outnumbered force of British troops ambushed and defeated a Spanish column, thwarting an attack on Frederica. A diorama of the Battle of Bloody Marsh depicts the story of this conflict.

French garrison guns are inspected by young visitors at Fort Frederica. Muzzle-loading smoothbore cannons similar to these were used for over 700 years.

The visitor center/museum stages live exhibits of military life at Fort Frederica.

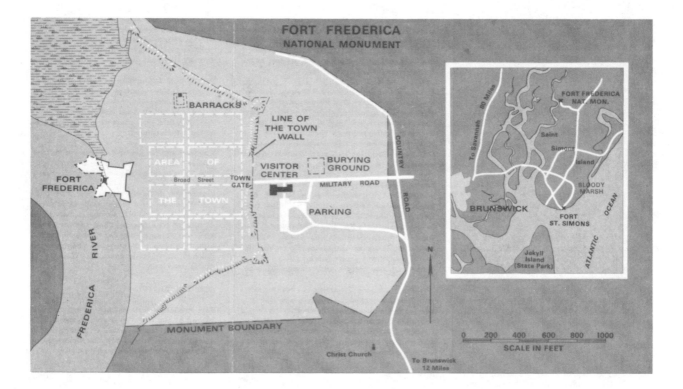

OLD FORT JACKSON

P.O. Box 782, Savannah, GA 31402
Telephone: (912) 232-3945
Director: Scott W. Smith
Hours: Tuesday through Sunday 9 A.M. to 5 P.M.;
closed Thanksgiving and Christmas
Cost of admission: Adults $1.50; military, students,
and retired people 75¢

Description: Fort Jackson, on the Savannah River, is the oldest fortification still standing in Georgia. The manmade brick walls were begun in 1808 under President Thomas Jefferson. These were times when the young country was struggling to remain neutral amid European wars of the Napoleonic era. First used during the War of 1812 with Great Britain, this fort was the key to Savannah's defense and stood as a sentinel before every ship that entered Savannah. In 1964 the state began physical restoration and opened it to the public in 1967. In 1975 the Coastal Heritage Society was formed as a private nonprofit organization to preserve it and provide interpretation for visitors.

Old Fort Jackson. Confederate militia as they would have looked in their ragtag outfits.

FORT PULASKI NATIONAL MONUMENT

P.O. Box 98, Tybee Island, GA 31328
Telephone: (912) 786-5787
Superintendent: Grady C. Webb
Hours: Daily 8:30 A.M. to 5:30 P.M.; summer 8:30
A.M. to 7 P.M.; closed Christmas
Cost of admission: $1 per car maximum summer only

Description: Visitor center museum exhibits include artifacts recovered from period of this site's major occupation from 1828 to 1880. Focal point is April 10–11, 1862, siege of Fort Pulaski when rifled cannons were first used successfully against masonry fortifications. Fort Pulaski is a living history museum, where visitors see examples of everyday life of a Civil War garrison. Several furnished rooms are open to the public on a rotation basis. Many examples of artillery including Blakely, Brooke, Parrott, and Columbiad cannons, are on display.

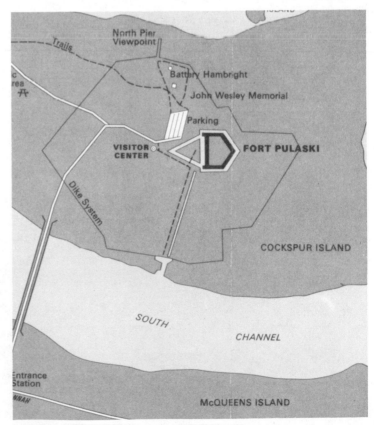

Aerial view of southeast angle of Fort Pulaski showing damage from April 10–11, 1862, siege.

U.S. ARMY MUSEUM, HAWAII

Fort Shafter, Waikiki, HI 96858
Telephone: (808) 543-2639
Director: Thomas M. Fairfull
Hours: Tuesday through Friday 10 A.M. to 4:30
P.M.; closed holidays
Cost of admission: Free to the public
Description: Artifacts reflecting the history of the Army in the Pacific, the military history of Hawaii, and the role played by Hawaii and Hawaiians in national defense are exhibited. The collection includes photographs of Schofield Barracks from 1910 to 1940, unit group pictures from the same period, and photos of the 25th Division in World War II, Korea, and Vietnam. Army manuals from 1910 to 1920 and archival materials dating back to the War of 1812 are also included. In addition, the museum displays the colors and guidons of units that have been stationed at Schofield, a variety of U.S. Army uniforms, and a collection of oil paintings depicting the 25th Division's activities in Vietnam. Exhibits show weapons captured by the 25th in various wars of the Pacific. There is also a collection of American pistols, rifles, machine guns, artillery, and tracked vehicles.

U.S. Army Museum by the beach at Waikiki, Honolulu, showing the outdoor gun park at Fort DeRussy.

The history of the U.S. Army in the Hawaiian Islands is depicted in the museum.

FORT SHERIDAN MUSEUM

Bldg. 33, Fort Sheridan, IL 60037
Telephone: (312) 926-2173 or 926-3520
Curator: Capt. Jenna
Hours: Tuesday through Saturday 10 A.M. to
4 P.M.; Sunday noon to 4 P.M.; closed Christmas
and New Year's Day
Cost of admission: Free to the public

Description: Fort Sheridan is 25 miles north of Chicago. The museum displays the notable achievements of the fort and the U.S. Army. The collection includes a Germantown Rockaway Carriage; many American and foreign flags (including a thirteen-star flag); military paintings; a group of military miniatures; the Lenox Lohr assemblage of over 100 weapons and other items used in World War I; a wide assortment of firearms, edged weapons, machine guns, mor-

The Fort Sheridan Museum has an extensive collection of small arms from all periods of American history.

tars, and missiles; a large display of uniforms dating back to 1860; an exhibit of military music; foreign military equipment; and medical equipment including instruments and a medical kit used during the Civil War.

A Germantown Rockaway Carriage, for the commanding general's use, is on display along with many other rare items used by the military before and after the Civil War.

PIETHMAN MUSEUM

Fort de Chartres State Historic Site, Praire du Rocher, IL 62277
Telephone: (618) 284-7230
Site Superintendent: Dorrell Duensing
Hours: Monday through Friday 8:30 A.M. to 5 P.M.; weekends 9 A.M. to 5 P.M.; closed Thanksgiving and New Year's Day

Cost of admission: Free to the public
Description: The museum deals with the 18th-century life at Fort de Chartres. Exhibits show French military and civilian life at the fort, Indian social life, and English military life. There are many military artifacts and weapons, as well as civilian period artifacts, on display. The fort was built in 1720 and many of the military artifacts date back to its founding.

JOHN M. BROWNING MEMORIAL MUSEUM

Rock Island Arsenal, Government Bridge, Attn: SARRI-AB, Rock Island, IL 61201
Telephone: (309) 794-5021
Curator: Dorrell E. Jarrison
Hours: Wednesday through Saturday 11 A.M. to 4 P.M.; closed Thanksgiving, Christmas, and New Year's Day
Cost of admission: Free to the public
Description: The Browning Memorial Museum exhibits material sent to the Chief of Ordnance

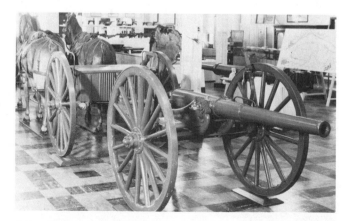

John M. Browning Memorial Museum. U.S. 3.2-inch field gun model of 1892. Carriage manufactured at Rock Island Arsenal, 1894.

for study and development, and numerous items illustrating the history of the Rock Island area, of the arsenal itself, and of U.S. Army weapons and equipment. The exhibits include bronze Revolutionary War field guns; both Union and Confederate muzzle-loading cannon; the first model of a metal field-gun carriage and limber made at Rock Island Arsenal, complete with four-horse hitch, harness, and equipment; a World War I French 75-mm field gun with limber; and a number of other artillery weapons. The museum also has an extensive collection of small arms.

105-mm Howitzer.

Winchester carbines, model 1866.

MEMORIAL HALL OF FLAGS

Centennial Bldg., 2nd and Edwards sts., Springfield, IL 62705

Telephone: (217) 785-3502

Historian/Curator: Charles W. Munie

Hours: Daily 8 A.M. to 4:30 P.M.

Cost of admission: Free to the public

Description: The glass cases along the north and south sides of the Hall of Flags contain 463 flags carried by Illinois regiments serving in 4 wars.

Hall of Flags, Springfield, Ill.

Displayed are 2 flags from the Mexican War, 346 from the Civil War, 22 from the Spanish-American conflict, and 93 from World War I. Many of the flags dated before 1900, especially those associated with the Civil War, were carried into battle. Soldiers in battle were told to watch their colors and move with them. Men who became separated from their units were told to rally around the flag. Since these flags were carried into battle, they were damaged. When the damage became too great they would be retired, and the regiment would receive a new set. A large number of our regiments have 2 sets on display, with some having as many as 3.

1ST DIVISION MUSEUM

1 S 151 Winfield Rd., Cantigny, Wheaton, IL 60187

Telephone: (312) 668-5161

Curator: CSM James Knox (Ret.)

Hours: Tuesday through Sunday, summer (Memorial Day to Labor Day) 9 A.M. to 5 P.M.; winter (Labor Day to Memorial Day) 10 A.M. to 4 P.M.; closed January

Cost of admission: Free to the public

Description: Cantigny is 30 miles west of the Chicago Loop via the Eisenhower Expy. and the East–West Tollway. Turn off north at Naperville Rd. to Butterfield Rd. Go west to Winfield Rd., then north to Cantigny. The 1st Division Museum tells with the aid of dioramas, spoken words, photographs, and artifacts the story of this famous division in the two World Wars and in Vietnam. The visitor goes at his own pace, pushing a button to start each display. To listen to and watch all displays requires about 2 hours. A reading room contains books and documents about the division. Outdoors near the front of the museum are 6 combat tanks representing types used in World War II, the Korean conflict, and Vietnam.

Cantigny, 1st Division Museum.

A full-scale reproduction of a World War I dugout.

38TH INFANTRY DIVISION MEMORIAL MUSEUM

431 N. Meridian, Indianapolis, IN 46204
Telephone: (317) 635-1964
Director: Col. William A. Scott, AUS (Ret.)
Hours: Tuesday through Sunday 9 A.M. to 4 P.M.;
closed holidays
Cost of admission: Free to the public
Description: The 38th Infantry Division Memorial Museum is located in the lower level of the War Memorial Building in Indianapolis. Dedicated to all the men and women who have served in the 38th Division of the Indiana National Guard and its lineal antecedents, it is a monument to the spirit of the militia that has played such a large part in winning and preserving this nation's freedom. It is a memorial Hoosiers may regard with considerable pride as a fitting tribute to those militiamen who have made the supreme sacrifice. The visitor enters the 38th Infantry Museum after passing through the general military museum in the lower level of the War Memorial. Inside the entrance is a 6-feet-tall bronze statue of a modern-day National Guard infantryman. Exhibits are arranged in chronological order. They represent units back through the territorial period to 1800.

Entrance to 38th Infantry Division Memorial Museum.

World War I display.

U.S. FINANCE CORPS MUSEUM

Army Finance and Accounting Center, Indianapolis, IN 46249
Telephone: (317) 542-2441
Curator: William Carnes
Hours: Monday through Friday 8 A.M. to 4 P.M.;
closed holidays
Cost of admission: Free to the public
Description: Exhibits include payrolls, claims, collection, and expenditure vouchers; pay tables; ledger cards; transportation accounts; deposit books, articles, clippings, letters, scrapbooks, memoirs, regulations, and financial manuals; photographs and pictures; American Continental notes of 1777 and 1780; military scrip

and military payment certificates and related historical documents and data; plus various mementos of Army finance activities and personnel. Included are currency of China, Korea, Japan, South America, the Middle East, South-east Asia, the Philippines, Vietnam, and European countries; U.S. and Allied invasion and liberation notes; World War II POW canteen chits; and Korean and Philippine counterfeit money.

Finance Corps Museum, view of east side of north lobby.

GEORGE ROGERS CLARK NATIONAL HISTORICAL PARK

401 S. 2nd St., Vincennes, IN 47591

Telephone: (812) 882-1776

Hours: Daily 8:30 A.M. to 5 P.M.; closed

Thanksgiving, Christmas, and New Year's Day

Cost of admission: Free to the public

Description: The entrance to the park is on 2nd St. south of U.S. 50. The park preserves the site of Fort Sackville, the approaches to the Lincoln Memorial Bridge, and the Buffalo Trace crossing of the Wabash River into Illinois. The memorial commemorates the George Rogers Clark expedition of 1778–79 and its decisive consequences on the winning of the Old Northwest. Near the memorial the white-spired St. Francis Xavier Church is a prominent reminder of French religious roots that were as important to the beginnings of the American nation as the Protestant energies behind English expansion

The George Rogers Clark Memorial, on the site of old Fort Sackville in Vincennes, Ind., commemorates the George Rogers Clark Expedition of 1778–79 that helped in the winning of the Old Northwest.

across the Appalachians. During the opening years of the American Revolution, the British dominated the old Northwest from their military post at Detroit. In 1777, the Americans found a man who would end Britain's dominance of the region, George Rogers Clark. This museum tells the story of Clark's expedition into the Northwest.

The visitor center displays an assortment of Revolutionary War military equipment, such as weapons, uniforms, and frontier maps.

FORT ATKINSON MUSEUM

North of Fort Atkinson, IA 52144
Telephone: (319) 534-7543
Curator: Mrs. Lois Rausch
Hours: Daily 9 A.M. to 5 P.M.
Cost of admission: Free to the public
Description: Fort Atkinson is in Winneshiek County on Hwy. 24 just north of the town of the same name. On May 31, 1840, Capt. Isaac Lynd,

with 71 men and officers of the 5th Infantry, arrived at Fort Atkinson. By the spring of 1841, it was clear that foot soldiers could not cope with the restless Winnebagos. Small bands were continually returning to Wisconsin. Permission was then given to build stables and quarters for cavalry. On June 24, 1841, Company B, 1st Regiment of Dragoons, arrived at the post to do most of the patroling necessary to keep the Indians in bounds. Pictures, military artifacts, treaties, and the history of events are displayed by the museum.

FORT LEAVENWORTH MUSEUM

Reynolds and Gibbon aves., Fort Leavenworth, KS 66027
Telephone: (913) 684-3191 or 684-3553
Curator: Griffith G. Gates
Hours: Monday through Saturday 10 A.M. to 4 P.M.; Sunday and holidays noon to 4 P.M.; closed Thanksgiving, Christmas, New Year's Day, and Easter

The Fort Leavenworth Museum was established in 1937 and moved into this building in 1959. It contains the largest collection of 19th-century horsedrawn military vehicles in the country.

Cost of admission: Free to public; donations welcome

Description: Fort Leavenworth and its museum are adjacent to the city of Leavenworth, Kans. From I-70 take Bonner Springs/Leavenworth turnoff. Go 18 miles north on Rt. 73 to northern boundary of Leavenworth city. Continue on Rt. 73; go 3 blocks to first stoplight. Main entrance to Fort Leavenworth is on right at this intersection. The museum contains an outstanding collection of horse-drawn vehicles dating from mid 19th century to early 20th century. The collection is one of the most comprehensive in America and includes army wagons, family-type carriages, and coaches used for public transportation. One of the rare examples of an Army horse-drawn vehicle is the carriage used by Abraham Lincoln on his visit to Kansas in December 1859.

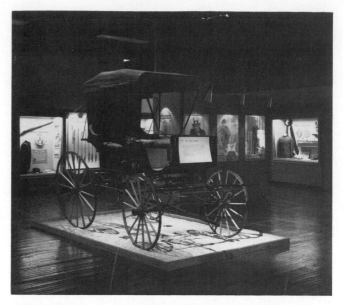

Called the Lincoln carriage, this carriage is a fine example of the quality workmanship put into horsedrawn vehicles.

U.S. CAVALRY MUSEUM

P.O. Box 9232, Fort Riley, KS 66442
Telephone: (913) 239-2737 or 239-2743
Curator: Terry Van Meter
Hours: Daily 10 A.M. to 4 P.M.; closed Christmas
Cost of admission: Free to the public

Description: The museum displays the history of the U.S. Cavalry, the post of Fort Riley, and the development of the American West. The cavalry museum is located in the traditional home of its branch. It exhibits the uniforms, weaponry, and equipment of the horse cavalry era, as well as books, maps, reference materials, and memorabilia. Its collections include a large number of U.S. military riding saddles, several works of art including an original Remington painting, an assortment of cavalry and dragoon weapons, and a group of cavalry training films produced by the museum.

The U.S. Cavalry Museum features harness, tack, and gear used by both man and beast.

FORT HARKER MUSEUM

Kanopolis, KS 67454
Telephone: (913) 472-4561
Curator: Clint Goodwin
Hours: Tuesday through Saturday, summer 10 A.M.
to noon, 1 P.M. to 5 P.M.
Cost of admission: Donations only
Description: What is now the city of Kanopolis had its beginning in 1864 when Lt. Allen Ellsworth and a company of men established Fort Ellsworth about 1½ miles south of this guardhouse museum. In November of 1866 Fort Ellsworth was abandoned and Fort Harker established. Early in the spring, Maj. Gen. Winfield S. Hancock arrived with a detachment of cavalry en route to New Mexico. He commanded the whole region. *Harper's Weekly* of April 27, 1867, on display at this museum, adds that on April 1, 2,000 men, including the 7th Cavalry commanded by Col. George Custer, with Gen. A. J. Smith as field commander of the entire unit went into camp on the Smoky Bottom just west of the post. "Wild Bill" Hickock was attached as a scout and "quite a number of

Fort Harker guardhouse.

Delaware Indians accompanied the command as scouts, hunters, and interpreters."

Fort Harker was built in order to guard the route of the Butterfield Overland Despatch and the Smoky Hill shortcut to Denver "which passed through the most Indian-infested region in Kansas."

Laborers on the Kansas Pacific Railroad tracks pause to eat fresh watermelon.

71

FORT LARNED NATIONAL HISTORIC SITE

Rt. 3, Larned, KS 67550
Telephone: (316) 285-3571
Superintendent: Jimmy D. Taylor
Hours: Daily 8 A.M. to 5 P.M.; early June to late
August 8 A.M. to 7 P.M.; closed Christmas
Cost of admission: Free to the public

Description: Located 6 miles west of the city of Larned on U.S. 156, Fort Larned was first charged with protecting the mail and travelers from attacks by the Plains Indians on the eastern leg of the Santa Fe Trail. Later it served as a center for attempts to administer Indian affairs peacefully, while at the same time it was a base for military operations against the Indians. Fort Larned's final task, which actually put an end to its usefulness, was to guard the construction crews that pushed the Santa Fe Railroad west across the plains. The railroad displaced the slower-moving, more vulnerable wagon traffic along the old trail. A museum located in the Visitors' Center depicts these exciting times with audiovisual displays, photographs, and artifacts. There are 6 other displays housed in as many reconstructed buildings.

Looking south to north down officers' row at Fort Larned.

A cavalryman on horseback gives Fort Larned visitors an insight into frontier military life.

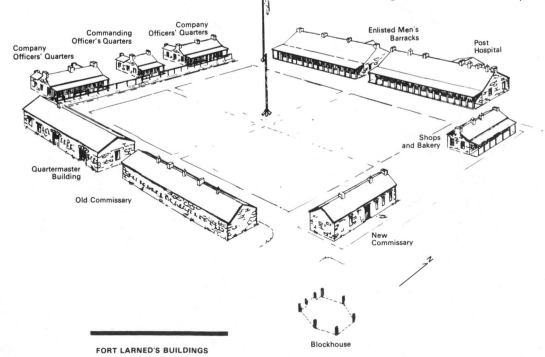

FORT LARNED'S BUILDINGS

DON F. PRATT MEMORIAL MUSEUM

Fort Campbell, KY 42223
Telephone: (502) 798-3215 or 798-4986
Curator: Joe D. Huddleston
Hours: Monday through Friday 12:30 to 4 P.M.;
weekends 1 P.M. to 4:30 P.M.; closed Christmas Eve,
Christmas, and New Year's Day
Cost of admission: Free to the public

Description: Fort Campbell, Ky., is 5 miles north of Clarksville, Tenn. From Nashville take Rt. Alt. 41 (41A) north 50 miles to Fort Campbell main gate. The museum is in Wickham Hall at 26th and Tennessee Ave., 1 mile from main gate. The building houses more than 70 exhibits representing, in part, the history of the U.S. Army. Dedicated in honor of the 101st Airborne Division's first assistant division commander, the museum features exhibits that portray the gallant history of the Screaming Eagles from 1942 to the present. Displays regress in time from a helicopter to tiny arrowheads. Weapons, photographs, and equipment are used to illustrate the almost 7 years of combat operations by the division in Korea. The Buffalo Soldier exhibit depicts black history of the old West. The 9th and 10th Cavalry served with distinction in the 1866–98 period.

The Don F. Pratt museum building, Fort Campbell, Ky.

PATTON MUSEUM OF CAVALRY AND ARMOR

P.O. Box 208, Fort Knox, KY 40272
Telephone: (502) 634-6350
Curator: Philip M. Cavanaugh
Hours: Daily 9 A.M. to 4:30 P.M.; May through
September 9 A.M. to 6 P.M.
Cost of admission: Free to the public

Description: Fort Knox is 36 miles southwest of Louisville, Ky. From Louisville proceed south on Rt. 31W for 36 miles to Chaffee Ave. turnoff; take turnoff to main gate of Fort Knox. Museum is at the main gate. It contains memorabilia of the late Gen. George S. Patton, Jr., and includes his ivory-handled revolvers as well as the 1939 Cadillac he was riding in at the time of the accident that led to his death. Museum also possesses a large collection of weapons and uniforms of tankers of all nations, as well as a great number of armored vehicles from numerous countries. The museum portrays the evolution, history, and traditions of the U.S. Cavalry and Armor.

The museum building that tells the story of Gen. George S. Patton, Jr., hero of World War II.

Lt. Gen. George S. Patton, Jr., salutes troops under his command as they pass in review during an inspection tour in Armagh, Northern Ireland, April 3, 1944.

KENTUCKY MILITARY HISTORY MUSEUM

c/o Kentucky Historical Society,
P.O. Box H, E. Main St., Frankfort, KY 40602
Telephone: (502) 564-3265
Curator: Nicky Huges
Hours: Daily 9 A.M. to 4 P.M.; Sunday 1 P.M. to 5
P.M.; closed Thanksgiving, Christmas, and New
Year's Day
Cost of admission: Free to the public

Description: Collection contains materials related to Kentucky's military history, with emphasis upon Kentucky's Militia, National Guard, and other volunteer units; several hundred firearms including large automatic-weapons collection; also uniforms, flags, photographs, documents, personal items, medals, and decorations. Main exhibit series is "Kentucky in Uniform," a chronologically arranged interpretation of all aspects of Kentucky's role in U.S. military history; highlights include silver service from the USS *Kentucky*, Kentucky Rifles, artillery pieces from the Revolution through World War II, large Civil War collection; library. Building housing these treasures is the Old State Arsenal constructed in 1850.

Kentucky Military History Museum staff member prepares temporary exhibit of decorations of Maj. Gen. Edgar E. Hume, Frankfort, Ky. Hume received over 130 decorations from nations around the world during his career as a U.S. Army medical officer. This temporary exhibit was one of a series of such exhibits constantly under way at the museum.

Exhibit of the silver service from the battleship U.S.S. *Kentucky* (BB6). This service was purchased by the people of Kentucky for the ship in 1900. It was returned to Kentucky in the 1920s following the decommissioning of the ship. The naval officer's uniform pictured was owned by Adm. Charles Duncan, Nicholasville, Ky., former Supreme Allied Commander, Atlantic (NATO).

CUMBERLAND GAP NATIONAL HISTORICAL PARK

P.O. Box 840, Middlesboro, KY 40965

Telephone: (606) 245-2817

Superintendent: Thomas L. Hartman

Hours: Daily 8 A.M. to 5 P.M.; summer 8 A.M. to 7 P.M.; closed Christmas

Cost of admission: Free to the public

Description: Cumberland Gap contains over 20,000 acres in the states of Kentucky, Virginia, and Tennessee. It can be reached by taking U.S. 25E from Kentucky and Tennessee or U.S. 58 from Virginia. Visitor center/museum contains a wide variety of combat artifacts taken from this area during the Revolutionary and Civil wars. Sound/slide programs and exhibits represent the oftentimes violent history of the Gap from prehistoric Indian activity to modern times. Included are exhibits depicting the Civil War occupation of the Gap and its significant strategic value during the first 3 years of the war. A field museum at Hensley Settlement represents a modern "pioneer" community. This is Daniel Boone country and many of the exhibits extol the accomplishments of this wonderful frontiersman.

The Willie Gibbons house, a typical dwelling for both civilian and soldier. Cumberland Gap National Historical Park.

A 24-pound Civil War siege cannon. Many such weapons dot the historic land surrounding the visitor center/museum.

PERRYVILLE BATTLEFIELD STATE SHRINE

Rt. 1, Old Mackville Rd., Perryville, KY 40468
Telephone: (606) 332-8631
Curator: Elizabeth C. Barker
Hours: April 1 through October 31 9 A.M. to 5 P.M.
Cost of admission: Adults 75¢; children 25¢; adult groups of 10 or more 50¢
Description: Located in Boyle County near Hwys.

U.S. 68 and 150, this historic site and museum marks the site of the Battle of Perryville, fought on October 8, 1862. The Confederate Army of 16,000 under the leadership of Gen. Braxton Bragg had advanced into Kentucky to obtain supplies and to enlist dissatisfied Kentuckians. The powerful Union Army of 61,000 caught up with them and forced a stand. Gen. Don Carlos Buell ordered 22,000 of his men into battle with the Confederates. Over 6,000 of the Blue and Gray were killed, wounded, or missing by nightfall.

CHALMETTE NATIONAL HISTORICAL PARK

P.O. Box 429, Arabi, LA 70032
Telephone: (504) 271-2412
Hours: Daily 8 A.M. to 5 P.M.; closed Christmas, New Year's Day, and Mardi Gras
Cost of admission: Free to the public

Description: America won a brilliant victory here in the Battle of New Orleans during the War of 1812. The park includes Chalmette National Cemetery, with 15,291 interments, of which 6,773 are unidentified. The visitors' center at the park contains battlefield artifacts, muskets, cannonballs, a small diorama of the American line at Chalmette, a helmet, drum, unit patches, displays, wall-mounted pictures, and information about the action.

The beautiful visitor center/museum at Chalmette National Historical Park stands in St. Bernard Parish, on the east side of the Mississippi River, still protected by its Civil War cannons.

FORT POLK MILITARY MUSEUM

Bldg. 917, P.O. Drawer R, Fort Polk, LA 71459
Telephone: (318) 537-7905
Curator: George S. Hammerschmidt
Hours: Monday through Friday 8 A.M. to 4 P.M.;
weekends 8 A.M. to 5 P.M.; holidays 8 A.M. to 5
P.M.; closed Thanksgiving, Christmas, and New
Year's Day

Cost of admission: Free to the public
Description: While the collection covers U.S. Army history from the American Revolution to the present, its primary emphasis is the period from World War II to the present, and it highlights histories of units that are or have been stationed at Fort Polk since its activation in 1941. A 2½-acre outdoor museum park features over 75 major items of armor, aviation, ordnance, engineer, and artillery equipment.

MANSFIELD STATE COMMEMORATIVE AREA

Rt. 2, Box 252, Mansfield, LA 71052
Telephone: (318) 872-1474
Historic Site Manager 1: G. B. Edge
Hours: Daily 9 A.M. to 5 P.M.; Sundays 1 to 5
P.M.; closed Thanksgiving, Christmas, and New
Year's Day
Cost of admission: Adults $1, over 62 years free;
students 50¢

Description: The area is located in DeSota Parish, 4 miles south of the town of Mansfield on La. 175. Interesting attractions for visitors to the museum include an electric map showing General Banks' march up the Red River, two dioramas of the campaign with tape-recorded commentary, a collection of weapons, firing arms, explosives, and bullets found on the battlefield, old uniforms, and other historical artifacts.

An extensive library of books and documents exclusively relating to the Civil War is also housed in the Museum Building. There are 128 volumes of the War of Rebellion Union and Confederate Armies, 10 volumes of official records of the Union and Confederate Navy, 4 volumes of records of Louisiana Confederate Soldiers, plus historic letters, books, diaries, and documents.

Civil War soldier.

80

Cannon in front of museum and some of the monuments in front of the park at Mansfield State Commemorative Area.

FORT JESUP

Rt. 2, Many, LA 71449
Telephone: (318) 256-5480
Superintendent: W. D. Manasco
Cost of admission: Free to the public
Description: Fort Jesup State Commemorative

Area is located 6 miles east of the city of Many on La. 6, formerly the original El Camino Real. The story of this fort is told in its museum with the use of maps, documents, and illustrations. A diorama shows the fort under construction in the 1830s. Military artifacts of the period round out the collection. The commanding officer's bedroom is furnished as it would have been

Replica of the officers' quarters at Fort Jesup.

Interior of army kitchen.

when Gen. Zachary Taylor slept there in 1845. The United States built Fort Jesup in 1822. The army quickly established law and order in the

Sabine Strip, and Fort Jesup remained an important military post until it was no longer needed and hence abandoned in 1845.

CONFEDERATE MUSEUM

929 Camp St.,
New Orleans, LA 70130
Telephone: (504) 523-4522
Curator: Mrs. Belinda Reuther
Hours: Daily 10 A.M. to 4 P.M.
Cost of admission: Adults $1; students 50¢; children 25¢

Description: Just off Lee Circle, not too far from Canal St., this memorial to the Confederacy is the oldest museum in Louisiana. Established in 1891, the museum exhibits thousands of priceless mementos of the War between the States. This museum has been characterized as one of the best of its kind. Exhibits consist of many rare paintings, the original uniform of Gen. P. G. T. Beauregard, numerous historic battle flags, a wide variety of weapons, medical instruments of the day, the silver service used by Robert E. Lee, and many other unusual military items. The museum contains two rare stained-glass windows. One honors the "Chaplain of the Confederacy," Fr. Abram J. Ryan, Southern poet as

The Confederate Museum building is well marked by the 10-inch Rodman Civil War cannon that sits to the right of the entrance.

well as chaplain. A raised platform is devoted to memorabilia of Jefferson Davis, only President of the Confederacy, and of his wife and their daughter, Winnie Davis.

FORT PIKE STATE COMMEMORATIVE AREA

Rt. 6, Box 194, New Orleans, LA 70129
Telephone: (504) 662-5703
Curator: Charles Bendzans,
Hours: Daily 9 A.M. to 5 P.M.
Cost of admission: Adults $1; children 50¢; senior citizens and children under 7 years free
Description: Fort Pike Area is located adjacent to the Old Spanish Trail (U.S. 190), approximately

23 miles east of New Orleans. The fort, set on a 125-acre site, was constructed shortly after the War of 1812 to defend navigational channels leading into the city of New Orleans. Fort Pike is a museum in itself, for visitors can stroll through authentic bricked archways and stand overlooking the Rigolets as sentries once did. Fort Pike was named in honor of American Brig. Gen. Zebulon Montgomery Pike (1779–1813), whose mark in history is also recognized at Pike's Peak, the Rocky Mountain peak he and his expedition reached in 1806.

LOUISIANA MILITARY HISTORY AND STATE WEAPONS COLLECTION MUSEUM

Jackson Barracks, 6437 St. Claude Ave., New Orleans, LA 70117
Telephone: (504) 271-6262, Ext. 242 or 243
Director: Lt. Col. Robert Henderson, Jr., AUS (Ret.)
Hours: Monday through Friday 8 A.M. to 4 P.M.; or by appointment
Cost of admission: Free to the public
Description: The indoor display area exhibits muskets, rifles, carbines, machine guns, pistols, swords, sabers, bayonets, mortars, inert ammunition, artillery, flags, art, uniforms, individual equipment, U.S. Army staff car model 1917 Cadillac, wagon ambulance c. 1870, cavalry soldier and horse equipment. The outdoor display area has tanks, armored cars, armored personnel carriers, half-tracks, DUKW artillery, Multiple Gun Motor Carriage M-19 (twin 40-mm Bofors antiaircraft artillery guns mounted on

Cavalry wagon, tack, and weapons, World War I era.

modified light tank carriage M-24), Multiple Gun Motor Carriage M-13 (quad-mounted, air-cooled, .50-caliber machine gun in Maxton turret in rear of half-track M-3). These are things for the kids to climb on.

U.S. ARMY ORDNANCE MUSEUM

ATSL-DOSM, Aberdeen Proving Ground, MD 21005
Telephone: (304) 278-3602 or 278-5804
Curator: Daniel E. O'Brien
Hours: Tuesday through Friday noon to 3:45 P.M.; Saturday and Sunday 10 A.M. to 3:45 P.M.; closed Thanksgiving, Christmas, and New Year's Day
Cost of admission: Free to the public
Description: Turn right off U.S. 40 at the south end of Aberdeen, Md., onto Maryland Blvd. and proceed to the Military Police gate. This museum offers the most comprehensive collection of ordnance material in existence today. Since the material is representative of both United States and foreign design, it tells the full story of

Front entrance to Army Ordnance Museum.

modern ordnance development. The collection consists of nearly 18,000 pieces—small arms, artillery, combat vehicles, ammunition, body armor, and many other priceless items, including the rare and unusual. Although the main emphasis is directed toward weapons of the smokeless powder era, significant earlier items are among the museum's artifacts.

Staff car for Gen. John J. Pershing, commander-in-chief, American Expeditionary Force, World War I.

Sp4 Leroy Stratford, formerly of the Ordnance Museum staff, models an 1870s U.S. Army sergeant major (Ordnance Department) uniform. It is interesting to note that at this time, 1870–90, the Ordnance Corps was the only department in which a black could achieve a rank as high as sergeant major.

FORT MC HENRY NATIONAL MONUMENT AND HISTORIC SHRINE

End of E. Fort Ave., Baltimore, MD 21230
Telephone: (301) 962-4290
Hours: Daily 9 A.M. to 5 P.M.; Memorial Day 9 A.M. to 8 P.M.; closed Christmas and New Year's Day
Cost of admission: Free to the public

Description: Fort McHenry is 3 miles from the center of Baltimore, Md., and is readily accessible over E. Fort Ave., which intersects Md. 2. The successful defense of this fort in the War of 1812, September 13–14, 1814, saved the city of Baltimore from British destruction and inspired Francis Scott Key to write "The Star-Spangled Banner." Several of its buildings contain displays pertaining to the history of this area. The fort has been restored to its pre-Civil War appearance and restoration is constantly taking place. The flagstaff from which the flag flies 24 hours a day, by presidential proclamation, is in the exact location as the original. It was on the morning of the 14th that Key saw the flag still flying above the fort and knew the Americans were victorious. The poem he wrote on that occasion was published the next day and was soon being sung to the tune "To Anacreon in Heaven." The song was made the national anthem of the United States in 1931.

U.S. Marines perform a summer tattoo ceremony beneath Fort McHenry's replica "Star-Spangled Banner."

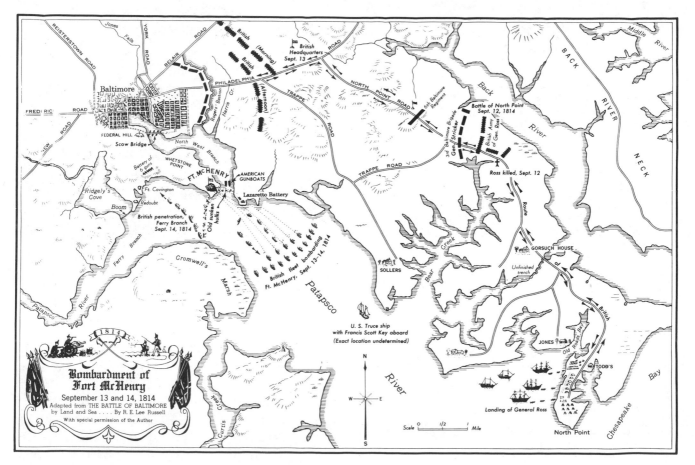

Bombardment of Fort McHenry.

Successful defense of Fort McHenry in the War of 1812 inspired Francis Scott Key to write "The Star-Spangled Banner." It never again came under enemy fire, although it continued to function as an active military post for the next 100 years.

FORT FREDERICK STATE PARK

P.O. Box 1, Big Pool, MD 21711
Telephone: (301) 842-2504
Park Manager: Paul W. Sprecher
Hours: Memorial Day to Labor Day 9 A.M. to 6
P.M.; or by appointment
Cost of admission: Free to the public; during special events, $2 per car, with varying charges for buses
Description: Fort Frederick can be found south of Rt. 40, west of Hagerstown and in the vicinity of Clear Springs and Indian Springs. Artifacts unearthed by archeological investigations since the 1930s are on display. The fort is now partially restored to its French and Indian War appearance. Reconstructed barracks contain furnished rooms depicting frontier military lifestyle of the 1750s. Living history features are demonstrated with interpreters dressed in 18th-century military and civilian clothing. The colony of Maryland built the fort during the French and Indian Wars (1754–63) to protect its western frontier. During the Revolutionary War the fort served as an American prison camp

Aerial view of Fort Frederick.

West barracks with room refurnished to appear as it did in 1758.

for captured British and German troops. A company of Union soldiers briefly manned its ruined walls during the Civil War. They fought a skirmish with raiders on Christmas Day 1861. The present state park began development in 1922.

FORT GEORGE G. MEADE MUSEUM

Attn.: AFZI-PTS-P, Fort George G. Meade, MD 20755

Telephone: (301) 677-6966

Curator: David C. Cole

Hours: Wednesday through Saturday 11 A.M. to 4 P.M.; Sunday 1 P.M. to 4 P.M.; closed federal holidays

Cost of admission: Free to the public

Description: Fort Meade is 15 miles northeast of Washington, D.C. Take Rt. 1 from Washington or Baltimore; at Rt. 198, turn east toward Laurel, which leads into Fort Meade. Turn right on Maples Rd. (still Rt. 198), continue to third traffic light, turn right on Griffin Ave. to museum. The Fort Meade museum contains exhibits showing the history of Fort Meade from World War I to the present. Exhibits show weapons, uniforms, and equipment of the U.S. Army as used at Fort Meade during this time. The mission of the museum also includes the history of the First United States Army, and its uniforms and memorabilia from World War I and World War II. Other exhibits display rare items, such as a World War I Renault tank, a Mark VIII tank, and an M3A1 scout car used during the late 1930s. In addition, the museum also houses a collection of research and experimental equipment.

The Fort Meade Museum has recently been reopened after reconstruction.

A World War I tank in the gun park outside the museum.

88

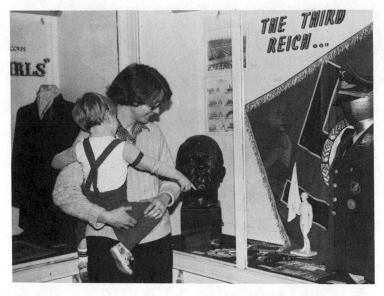

Nazi memorabilia at the Fort Meade Museum.

GATHLAND MUSEUM

900 Arnoldstown Rd., Jefferson, MD 21755
Telephone: (301) 293-2420
Curator: Ralph Young
Hours: Weekends and holidays 10 A.M. to 6 P.M.; or
by appointment
Cost of admission: Free to the public
Description: The museum features Civil War
artifacts—guns, bullets, items of uniform—and
books by George Alfred Townsend, the youngest war correspondent in the Civil War. Using
the pen name of Gath, he served both at home
and abroad, and later became one of America's
most important journalists and novelists of the
Reconstruction era.

Archway entrance to park near Gathland Museum.

FORT WASHINGTON MUSEUM

Fort Washington Park, 5210 Indian Head Hwy.,
Oxon Hill, MD 20021
Telephone: (301) 292-2112
Site Manager: Al Korzan
Hours: Fort, daily; museum, daily, June 1 to Labor
Day 8 A.M. to 8 P.M.; weekends and holidays 8 A.M.
to 5 P.M. Winter: 8:45 A.M. to 5:30 P.M.

Cost of admission: Free to the public
Description: Fort Washington is on the Maryland
side of the Potomac River. You can reach the
fort from Washington, D.C., by crossing the S.
Capitol St. Bridge and driving south on I-295
and east on I-495. Turn right onto Indian Head
Hwy. (Md. 210) and again right onto Fort
Washington Rd. This fort is an outstanding
example of early-19th-century coastal defense.
It was designed to withstand attack by wooden
naval vessels armed with smooth-bore artillery.

Its high masonry walls, gun positions, dry moat, and drawbridge illustrate some of the principles of military science and architecture used during our nation's early life. Fort Washington also occupies the site of the earliest fortification erected for the defense of the national capital. Picnic sites are available.

Drawbridge over dry moat, on land side, offered protection from attack.

An array of artillery used at Fort Washington.

POINT LOOKOUT STATE PARK VISITORS CENTER

Star Rt. Box 48, Scotland, MD 20687
Telephone: (301) 872-5688
Curator: Donald F. Hammett
Hours: Wednesday through Saturday 10 A.M. to 7:30 P.M.; winter hours vary
Cost of admission: Free to the public
Description: Point Lookout State Park is located at the southernmost tip of St. Mary's County, where the Potomac empties into Chesapeake Bay. The park entrance is reached via Rt. 5. Approximate driving time from Washington, D.C., is 2 hours; from Baltimore, Md., it is 2½ hours. Over 1,000 square feet of museum space contains 12 exhibits that tell of Point Lookout's Civil War history. Displays focus on Civil War

Point Lookout, Md., as it was during the Civil War when used as a POW encampment. At one time it held over 20,000 Confederate soldiers.

medicine, the black soldier in the Civil War, Civil War prisons and prisoners, and numerous artifacts found at Point Lookout. After the battle of Gettysburg in 1863, one area was developed as a prison. The facilities of the prison were inadequate for the great number of men confined. As a result, the captives were provided with only the barest essentials of life, poorly clad, poorly fed, and medically neglected. By April 1865 the prisoners at Point Lookout numbered 20,110 men—more men than General Lee had in his last army.

ANTIETAM NATIONAL BATTLEFIELD SITE

P.O. Box 158, Sharpsburg, MD 21782
Telephone: (301) 432-5124
Curator: Betty J. Otto
Hours: June through August 8 A.M. to 6 P.M.;
September through May 8:30 A.M. to 5 P.M.; closed
Thanksgiving, Christmas, and New Year's Day
Cost of admission: Free to the public

Description: Visitor center is 1 mile north of Sharpsburg off Hagerstown/Sharpsburg Pike (65). Gen. Robert E. Lee's first invasion of the North ended on this battlefield in 1862. The museum depicts how the general concentrated forces at Frederick, then sent Jackson's corps south to take Harpers Ferry and Longstreet's westward across the mountain. What resulted is explained through sound boxes, motion pictures, slides, and displays. Estimated losses were 9,000 Confederates and 12,000 Federals. Many contemporary photographs show carnage, wreckage, and landscape ruin that were the outcome. Uniforms of both sides are on display, as are weapons, ammunition, provisions, medical instruments, and other residue of combat. An important part of this museum is the surrounding park, which consists of almost 4,000 acres. There is also a 12-acre federal cemetery connected with the park, complete with markers.

Near the visitor center/museum stands this impressive statue to all those who gave their lives at Antietam.

91

Confederate dead at Antietam. Both Brady and his assistant, O'Sullivan, were present at the battle. The shoes in the foreground were used as a signature in the manner of Whistler's butterfly.

Ambulance drill before the battle of Antietam. Note that the medical officer *(extreme right)* wears a sword and other sidearms. Today's medical doctors go unarmed.

ANCIENT AND HONORABLE ARTILLERY COMPANY

Armory, Faneuil Hall, Boston, MA 02109
Telephone: (617) 227-1638
Exec. Secretary: Maj. Charles F. Hoar, MSG
Cost of admission: Free to the public
Description: Faneuil Hall is known as "The Cradle of Liberty," and houses the oldest military organization in the western hemisphere, which is the Ancient and Honorable Artillery Company. In 1742 Peter Faneuil, a prosperous merchant of the "Towne of Boston," presented the town with a building to be used as a public market, which was named in his honor. Under the terms of a Capt. Robert Keayne, the founder of this company, the town was obliged to furnish an armory for the "Artillery Company," which is the Ancient and Honorable Artillery Company of today. This armory was originally in the

Museum of the Ancient and Honorable Artillery Company.

"Towne" House at the head of what is now State St. After completion of Faneuil Hall, the armory was removed to that building in 1746, where it has been the home of the company for over 200 years. There is a musket room, a military museum, a spacious and well-decorated committee room, and an armory proper.

MINUTE MAN NATIONAL HISTORIC PARK

P.O. Box 160, Concord MA 01742
Telephone: (617) 369-6993
Superintendent: Robert Nash
Hours: Much of this historic park is based on public
roads open the year round.
Cost of admission: Free to the public
Description: This area was the scene of fighting on April 19, 1775, which opened the American Revolution. The park includes North Bridge, Minute Man Statue, 4 miles of Battle Road between Lexington and Concord, and "The Wayside," Nathaniel Hawthorne's home. This area was designated as a National Historic Site

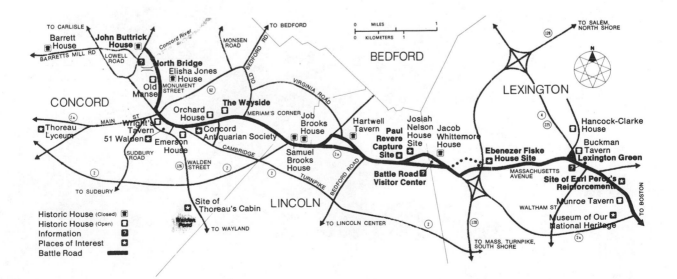

on April 14, 1959; changed to a National Historic Park on September 21, 1959. It consists of 745.37 acres. It was here, on Lexington Green, that a thin line of armed Americans marked the beginning of a new era in world history. Dec-

ades later one of these men who turned out to face the British explained his actions by saying, "We had always governed ourselves, and we always meant to."

SPRINGFIELD ARMORY NATIONAL HISTORIC SITE

1 Armory Square, Springfield, MA 01105
Telephone: (413) 734-8551
Curator: William E. Meuse
Hours: Daily 8 A.M. to 4:30 P.M.; closed
Thanksgiving, Christmas, and New Year's Day
Cost of admission: Free to the public
Description: This National Historic Site is located in the heart of Springfield, Mass., just off State St. Today, the words armory, arsenal, and magazine are often used interchangeably, but in the 18th and 19th centuries they had specific meanings. An armory was a place where arms were manufactured, an arsenal a place for storing the accouterments of war, and a magazine a storehouse for powder and ammunition. In its history Springfield Armory has served all of these functions. The weapons collection housed in the main arsenal was started about 1870 by Col. J. G. Benton as a "technical library" for armory personnel. It is now regarded as the world's largest collection of small arms.

Commandant's quarters, Springfield Armory.

Springfield Armory, main arsenal.

HISTORIC FORT WAYNE

6325 W. Jefferson Ave., Detroit, MI 48209
Telephone: (313) 849-0299
Curator: Dr. William P. Phenix
Hours: Wednesday through Saturday 9:30 A.M. to 5
P.M.; Sunday 11:30 A.M. to 7:30 P.M.; closed
December and March
Cost of admission: Adults $1
Description: This museum interprets Detroit's 2½

centuries of military history. Complete with dry moat, casemates, sally ports, tunnels, powder magazine, earthworks, and stone barracks, the fort represents the ultimate in classic military architecture. It was named in honor of Gen. Anthony Wayne, a veteran of the Revolutionary War and commander of the American forces that defeated the Indians at the Battle of Fallen Timbers in 1794. The fort remained a key garrison in the Spanish-American War and World War I. It served as a major ordnance and vehicle supply depot during World War II.

FORT MACKINAC

P.O. Box 370, Mackinac Island, MI 48909
Telephone: (906) 847-3328
Assistant Superintendent: David A. Armour
Hours: May 15 to June 15 10 A.M. to 4 P.M.; June
16 to Labor Day 9 A.M. to 6 P.M.
Cost of admission: spring and fall $2.50; June 16
through Labor Day $3; children under 12 years free
Description: There is much to be seen within Fort Mackinac: a post schoolhouse of 1879; the north blockhouse of 1798; post commandant's house of 1835; the hospital of 1828; the west blockhouse of 1798; a guardhouse of 1828; the officer's wooden quarters of 1800; the soldiers' barracks of 1859; an avenue of flags; a post bathhouse of 1885; the quartermaster's storeroom of 1867; the post headquarters of 1853; the south sally port, which leads to the city; the commissary of 1878; the east blockhouse of 1798; and the gun platforms. There are regularly scheduled guided tours, musket firings, and cannon salutes. The aim is to give an exact interpretation of fort life in the 19th century.

Musket shoots, cannon salutes, and demonstrations are all part of the Fort Mackinac Museum display.

The officers' stone quarters is only one of many exhibit buildings, each a museum unto itself.

FORT MICHILIMACKINAC

Mackinaw City, MI 49701
Telephone: (616) 436-5563
Curator: Keith Widder
Hours: May 15 to October 15; hours vary for different events
Cost of admission: spring and fall $2.50; June 16 to Labor Day $3

Description: Historic Fort Michilimackinac is an American Revolutionary War fortified town. The fort and its numerous buildings, the exhibits and period settings are the result of the most careful research of archeologists and historians to make this one of America's most authentic reconstructions. It is a living textbook. Fort Michilimackinac was built by the French in 1715. Many buildings on site depict the exciting past of this military establishment. Within its walls are a French trader's house, the church of St. Anne, a priest's house and blacksmith shop, a British trader's house, a water gate, a storehouse, a house for the commanding officer, a guardhouse, soldiers' barracks, and a powder magazine. Outside its walls are the Orientation Center and Maritime Park. Reconstruction of the site was begun in 1959 and has been going on ever since.

Main gate on land side of Fort Michilimackinac, guarded by sentry and cannon.

FORT RIDGELY

R.R. 1, Fairfax, MN 55332
Telephone: (507) 426-7469
Site Manager, Minnesota Historical Society: Lila Nesburg
Hours: Daily, May 1 to October 15, 10 A.M. to 5 P.M.
Cost of admission: Free to the public

Description: Fort Ridgely is located 7 miles south of Fairfax, Minn., off Minn. 4. An interpretive center is organized around key years in Fort Ridgely's history. A modern exhibit in the restored commissary tells visitors about life at an isolated military post in the middle years of the 19th century. A scale model shows how the fort looked in 1862, and an audiovisual program gives a complete account of the two battles that turned the tide of war in the Minnesota Valley. The role of Fort Ridgely and its garrison in the Dakota War cannot be overestimated. Many historians believe that the battles at Fort Ridgely and New Ulm settled the outcome of the war before it actually ended. "We thought the fort was the door to the valley as far as to St. Paul . . . but the defenders of the fort were very brave and kept the door shut," Chief Big Eagle, who had been present at the first battle, said later. "The cannon disturbed us greatly . . . but for the cannon I think we would have taken the fort."

The Fort Ridgely Interpretive Center's exhibits are organized around key years and events in the fort's history.

GRAND PORTAGE

P.O. Box 666, Grand Marais, MN 55604

Cost of admission: Free to the public

Description: Grand Portage National Monument is located off U.S. 61, 36 miles northeast of Grand Marais, Minn., 145 miles from Duluth and 45 miles southwest of the Canadian city of Thunder Bay, Ontario. The portage trail, included as part of the park, bisects the reservation of the Grand Portage Band of the Minnesota Chippewa Tribe. The portage trail winds through the woods to the site of Fort Charlotte, 8½ miles away on the Pugeon River. Fort Charlotte once was a way station for furs arriving from the Northwest in transit to the stockade at Grand Portage. To be seen are the company stockade, with palisades, blockhouse, and gates. Canoe Warehouse is a museum for authentic birch-bark canoes. A frontier kitchen and, the largest of the buildings, the Great Hall, where partners of the North West Company wrangled over furs, are open to visitors.

The "Scottie" Crawford cabin was the last cabin built at Grand Portage.

The largest of all buildings (now a museum) was the Great Hall. Here partners of the Northwest Company met to wrangle over business affairs, discuss the problem of Indians, and to make merry with dancing, singing, and playing of the bagpipes.

For at least 200 years the Indian birch-bark canoe served as the main transport in the fur trade. Here one of these famed craft is demonstrated at Grand Portage.

CAMP RIPLEY MUSEUM

Camp Ripley, Little Falls, MN 56345
Director: Adjutant General, State of Minnesota
Hours: June through August noon to 7 P.M.
Cost of admission: Free to the public
Description: General military items range from buttons to cannons and an old L-19 aircraft. Special emphasis is on the history of the citizen soldier in Minnesota. While the museum is under control of the Adjutant General, work is done by the Historical Committee, Minnesota National Guard Officers Association, and the Minnesota Historical Society. Major changes now taking place both to inside and outside of muscum building.

Main museum building, Camp Ripley.

L-19 observation plane in outside museum park.

HISTORIC FORT SNELLING

Bldg. 25, Fort Snelling, St. Paul, MN 55111
Telephone: (612) 726-9430
Director: Glenn Stille
Hours: Vary according to season of year
Cost of admission: Adults $1; children (6 to 16 years) 25¢
Description: Fort Snelling was once the last outpost of the U.S. authority in the northwestern wilderness. For almost 30 years Fort Snelling was the hub of the upper Mississippi—the center of government policy and administration and a haven for travelers who sought protection and society within its limestone walls. Fort Snelling is now a gateway to the past. Restored to its original appearance and staffed with costumed guides, the fort again opens its gate to welcome visitors. Officers still strut on the parade ground and soldiers still grumble about the hardships of army life in the 1820s.

GRAND GULF MILITARY MONUMENT MUSEUM

Rt. 2, Box 140, Port Gibson, MS 39150
Telephone: (601) 437-5911
Director: Mr. and Mrs. Phillip B. Cox
Hours: Tuesday through Saturday 8 A.M. to 5 P.M.; Sundays 10 A.M. to 6 P.M.; closed Thanksgiving, Christmas, New Year's Day
Cost of admission: Donations only
Description: This museum contains relics and artifacts from the Civil War and from the old town of Grand Gulf, which was once a large port on the Mississippi River. Its collections include home implements from the 1800s and early 1900s and a carriage house exhibited with carriages and other vehicles from the period. Perhaps no other town has played as significant a role in Mississippi history as has Grand Gulf—one-time boom town, theater center, and strategic Confederate stronghold during the Civil War. A virtual ghost town today, Grand Gulf has experienced success and failure such as few other communities anywhere.

The park is located 7 miles from Hwy. 61, northwest of Port Gibson, on the Mississippi River.

13-inch siege mortar.

Grand Gulf Military Monument Museum.

FORT MASSACHUSETTS

Ship Island, Mississippi

Cost of admission: Concession boat fares vary

Description: Access to Ship Island is provided by concession boats from Gulfport and Biloxi, Miss., twice daily May through September. In April, the only other month the boats operate, service is twice a day on weekends. Private boats may dock at Fort Massachusetts in the daytime. Ship Island has been two islands since 1969, when its middle section was washed away in a hurricane. The primitive campground on the eastern half can be reached only by boat.

Fort Massachusetts, Ship Island, Miss. At one time this fort could man a battery of 10 large coastal defense guns.

TUPELO NATIONAL BATTLEFIELD AND BRICES CROSS ROADS NATIONAL BATTLEFIELD SITE

Natchez Trace Pkwy., R.R. 1, NT-143, Tupelo, MS 38801

Telephone: (601) 842-1572

Superintendent: C. W. Ogle

Hours: Daily 24 hours

Cost of admission: Free to the public

Tupelo National Battlefield. View of monument and cannon from south edge of the site.

Description: Tupelo National Battlefield Site is within the city limits of Tupelo, Miss., on Miss. 6 about one mile west of its intersection with U.S. 45. It is 1.2 miles east of the Natchez Trace Pkwy. Brices Cross Roads Battlefield Site is located about 6 miles west of Baldwyn on Miss. 370. Critics of military tactics agree that the engagement was characterized by the hardest kind of fighting and was a brilliant tactical victory for Gen. Nathan Forrest, CSA. Despite this, the Battle at Brices Cross Roads did not bring relief to the Confederacy. Sherman, on this and other occasions, forestalled any attack on the Nashville-Chattanooga railroad. Assured of adequate supplies and reinforcements, he won the Atlanta campaign.

Union cavalry learned that Tupelo was unprotected, and on July 13, the Union forces headed in that direction. Realizing what was happening Forrest hurried up with his main force to attack the long Union column. The Northern soldiers beat off the attacks and marched on. At the little village, now within the Tupelo city limits, they camped, awaiting certain attack the next day. Thus was the battle brought about.

VICKSBURG NATIONAL MILITARY PARK

P.O. Box 349, Vicksburg, MS 39180
Telephone: (601) 636-0583
Superintendent: Daniel E. Lee
Hours: Daily 8 A.M. to 5 P.M.; summer 7 A.M. to 7 P.M.
Cost of admission: Free to the public
Description: Exhibits illustrate by use of portraits, dioramas, artifacts, and audiovisual programs, soldier and civilian life during the siege of Vicksburg. A film entitled *In Memory of Men* runs for 18 minutes and is shown on the hour and half hour. This film tells the story of the Vicksburg campaign. Living history demonstrations with artillery firing take place June through August. A special museum has been opened for the Union ironclad USS *Cairo*. This ship, ordered to destroy rebel batteries, steamed up the Yazoo River to carry out this mission. Suddenly, two explosions in quick succession tore gaping holes in the ship's bottom. Within 12 minutes the ironclad vanished. The hapless *Cairo* became the first vessel ever to be sunk by an electrically detonated mine, inaugurating a new era in naval warfare.

Opposing generals at Vicksburg.

Visitor center/museum, Vicksburg.

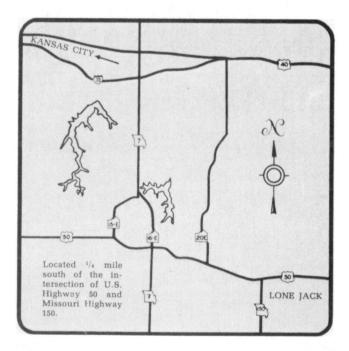

Shirley House, home of the Shirley family, Union sympathizers, which stood midway between the contending armies at the beginning of the siege. The house was badly damaged by shellfire but has since been restored. On the main floor are the superintendent's quarters and administration offices, and in the basement are the historical office and historical museum.

LONE JACK CIVIL WAR BATTLEFIELD MUSEUM

22807 Woods Chapel Rd., Blue Springs, MO 64015

Telephone: (816) 795-8200

Curator: Gary R. Toms

Hours: April through October, Monday, Tuesday and Friday 9 A.M. to 5 P.M.; March through December, Saturday and Sunday 9 A.M. to 5 P.M.

Cost of admission: Free to the public

Description: Displays include an electronic map of recorded account of Civil War activity in Jackson County, Mo.; dioramas depicting battles of Lone Jack and Westport, enforcement of Order #11, and Quantrill's raid on Lawrence, Kans.; as well as numerous exhibits relevant to the battle of Lone Jack and its commemoration. Museum is located on battlefield site, adjoining soldier's cemetery and remnant of ridge used as a defense. Jackson County, located on the western edge of the Missouri, was named in honor of Gen. Andrew Jackson. In 1854, the Kansas-Nebraska Act left the question of slavery up to the settlers of these two new territories. Jackson County wanted Kansas to have slavery, while the Abolitionists worked to make it a free state. Friction erupted into bloody border warfare. The beginning of the Civil War only served to increase the resentment and intensify the conflict.

LIBERTY MEMORIAL MUSEUM

100 W. 26th St., Kansas City, MO 64108

Telephone: (816) 274-1675

Curator: Mark L. Beveridge

Hours: Tuesday through Sunday 9:30 A.M. to 4:30 P.M.; closed Thanksgiving, Christmas, and New Year's Day

Cost of admission: Free to the public

Description: In Kansas City, Mo., the Liberty Memorial stands as a symbol "in perpetual memory of the courage, loyalty, and sacrifice, of the patriots who offered and gave their lives, their services, and their all, in defense of liberty." The Liberty Memorial Museum is the only major military museum specializing in the history of World War I and the part played by America in that war. The museum gallery has been completely revamped and the new exhibits include uniforms, weapons, insignia, and field equipment from all the armies of World War I. Large items on exhibit will include a British 5-

The Liberty Memorial Museum stands 358 feet above Station Plaza, with a diameter of 43 feet at the base.

inch deck gun, a German field howitzer, a U.S. escort wagon, and a new torpedo. Visitors will be able to go through a full-size replica of a trench as captured by the Americans in the Argonne Forest. Displays will also include artifacts from the aviation branch, the tank corps, and the U.S. forces in Russia during World War I.

PERSHING BOYHOOD HOME STATE HISTORIC SITE

State St. and Worlow St., Laclede, MO 64651
Telephone: (816) 963-2525
Administrator: Keith L. Graf
Hours: Monday through Saturday 10 A.M. to
4 P.M.; Sundays noon to 5 P.M.; closed
Thanksgiving, Christmas, New Year's Day, and
Easter
Cost of admission: Adults 50¢; children (6 to 12 years) 25¢
Description: Located in the heart of Laclede, Mo., this is the home of John J. Pershing, named General of the Armies after World War I by a special act of Congress. Pershing was born near Laclede and moved into this house with his family when he was 6. Here he lived during his twenty-first year, when he learned of his acceptance to the United States Military Academy at West Point. The nine-room house is furnished in the style of the late 19th century and includes

The General John J. Pershing home, Laclede, Mo.

a smokehouse and outdoor privy. Designated as a state historic site in 1952, the home is owned and maintained by the Missouri Department of Natural Resources, Division of Parks and Recreation.

WILSON'S CREEK NATIONAL BATTLEFIELD

Rt. 2, Box 75, Republic, MO 65738
Telephone: (417) 732-2903 or 732-2662
Hours: Daily 8:30 A.M. to 5 P.M.
Cost of admission: Free to the public
Description: The park is reached from U.S. 60 via Mo. M and ZZ and is located 3 miles east of Republic, Mo., and 10 miles southwest of Springfield. I-44 is 5 miles north. Museum contains Civil War items, such as cannon balls, musket balls, bayonets, reunion medals, flutes, a bed frame, a spinning wheel, and small library. The Battle of Wilson's Creek (called Oak Hill by the Confederates) was fought 10 miles southwest of Springfield, Mo., on August 10, 1861. Named for the stream that crosses the area where the battle took place, it was a bitter struggle between Union and Confederate forces for control of Missouri in the first year of the Civil War. Missouri's allegiance was of vital concern to the federal government. The state's strategic position on two vital waterways (the Missouri and Mississippi rivers), and its abundant manpower and natural resources made it imperative that Missouri remain with the Union.

Sign and cannon at entrance to Wilson's Creek National Battlefield.

SOLDIERS' MEMORIAL MILITARY MUSEUM

1315 Chestnut St., St. Louis, MO 63101

Telephone: (314) 622-4550

Curator: Larry L. Lanius

Hours: 9 A.M. to 5 P.M.

Cost of admission: Free to the public

Description: This memorial contains two museums, one on east side, the other on west side. At the entrance to each are modernistic aluminum light standards. Each museum has 7 glass

Wall case in east museum, World War II.

Entrance of south side of Soldiers' Memorial Military Museum.

Court of Honor, across the street from the memorial, dedicated in 1948 to those from the St. Louis area who lost their lives in World War II (2,573 names are engraved on the walls to the right). The monument in the foreground, dedicated in 1979, contains the names of the 214 who died in Vietnam. At the opposite end of the garden area is the Korean monument, also dedicated in 1979, with 153 names.

display cases set upon marble bases. The case frames are of aluminum, the case floors of American walnut. Four of the cases are 25 feet long, 3½ feet wide, and 3½ feet high. The cases contain relics and trophies picked up on the battlefields of various wars and brought to the United States by our returning soldiers. These include rifles, sidearms, machine guns, bay-onets, bombs, hand grenades, gas masks, swords, sabers, shells and shell cases, types of bullets, shrapnel, medals, flags, and other articles. There are 5 Congressional Medals of Honor on display, which is believed to be the largest collection exhibited anywhere to the public.

FORT OSAGE

4th and Osage sts., Sibley, MO 64015
Telephone: (816) 795-8200
Curator: Gary R. Toms
Hours: Monday through Friday 9 A.M. to 5 P.M.;
closed Thanksgiving, Christmas, and New Year's
Day
Cost of admission: Free to the public
Description: Fort Osage is a reconstructed fur
trade fort on original foundations. Built in 1808
by troops commanded by William Clark of the
Lewis and Clark expedition, it was occupied by
federal troops until 1827. The original building
party consisted of a company of 81 1st U.S.
Infantry, for garrison duty under Capt. Eli B.
Clemson, and a company of 80 St. Charles
Dragoons, mounted militia, who volunteered
their services to Gen. Clark for 30 days. The fort
served as part of the U.S. trade system with the
Indians until 1822. While supervising the building of the fort, William Clark requested the
Great and Little Osages to move their villages to
the immediate vicinity. At one time some 5,000
Indians settled about the fort. In 1825, the

View from upper level of blockhouse at Fort Osage.

Osage Treaty was signed, terminating the Osage
habitation in Jackson County, which was officially called a "county" in 1826. Artifacts and
memorabilia from these and other times are on
display.

CUSTER BATTLEFIELD NATIONAL MONUMENT

P.O. Box 39, Crow Agency, MT 59022
Telephone: (406) 638-2622
Curator: James Court
Hours: Daily 8 A.M. to 4:30 P.M.
Cost of admission: Free to the public
Description: Museum concentrates on Custer, the
Battle of the Little Big Horn, the Plains Indians,
and the Indian Wars. Shortly after the battle,
the field of combat became a popular tourist
attraction. Many easterners touring the northwest on the newly built Northern Pacific Railway
took time to journey up the Little Big Horn to
view the historic spot. Troops from Fort Custer,
which was established at the mouth of the Little
Big Horn in 1877, served as the first custodians.

Lt. Col. George A. Custer and his Indian scouts in
1873 on the Yellowstone Expedition.

In 1893, the War Department placed a superintendent in charge to protect the area from vandals and souvenir hunters. All of the early superintendents were retired soldiers; several of them had served in the northwestern Indian campaigns. What information was passed on to visitors depended on their imaginations. In 1886, on the tenth anniversary, several Army and Indian veterans of the fight returned to the battlefield for an elaborate observance. Prominent among them were Capt. Benteen, Lt. Godfrey, trumpeter Penwell, and Chief Gall of the Hunkpapa Sioux.

Those who fell were eventually buried in this hillside graveyard that now looks down on the modern visitor center/museum.

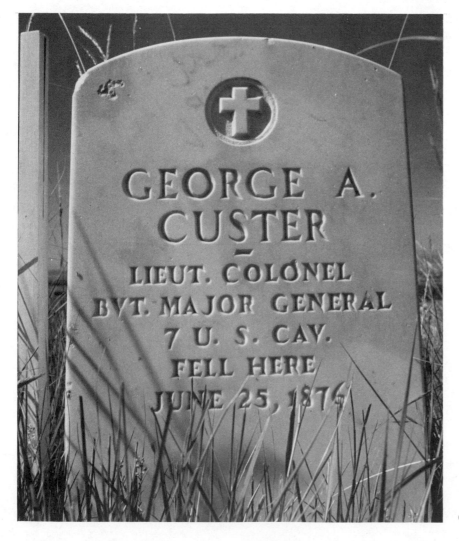

Custer headstone in Last Stand area.

FORT BENTON MUSEUM

1801 Front St., Fort Benton, MT 59442
Telephone: (406) 622-3311
Curator: Joel F. Overholster, P.O. Box 69, Fort Benton, MT 59442
Hours: Daily, June, July, August 10 A.M. to 7 P.M.
Cost of admission: Free to the public

Description: Fort Benton was founded in 1846 as an American fur trading post by Maj. Alexander Culbertson. The Fort Benton Museum is located in the Old Fort Park, is open June, July, and August, and at other times by appointment. Work on the museum was started in 1957 as a community enterprise using volunteer workers and maintained by the Community Improvement Association. The displays depict the early history of the Fort Benton area. It is also a regional museum as Fort Benton's role as a trade and transportation center involved much of the history of Montana, the northwestern

Entrance to the Fort Benton Museum.

U.S., and western Canada from the 1840s until 1887. A display in the museum also calls attention to 5 of Fort Benton's high-ranking military men, 2 generals and 3 admirals.

BIG HOLE NATIONAL BATTLEFIELD

P.O. Box 237, Wisdom, MT 59761
Telephone: (406) 689-2530
Hours: Daily 8 A.M. to 5 P.M.
Cost of admission: Free to the public

Description: Big Hole National Battlefield is 12 miles west of Wisdom, Mont., on Mont. 43. Visitors Center contains exhibits dating from the Nez Percé Indian War period, and reveal the conflicting cultures of the participants and the tragedy of the confrontation. The battle began at the Nez Percé camp, when soldiers surprised the sleeping Indians. The siege area, a wooded section, is also preserved, for it was here

A visitor center/museum at Big Hole National Battlefield contains military artifacts from the battlefield and explains the course of events before, during, and after the conflict. Col. John Gibbon, with a force of 182 men from the 7th Infantry, succeeded in sneaking up on 125 Indian warriors and their families. The battle of Big Hole ensued. It was here the Indians won the battle but lost the war, for their losses caused them to surrender 2 months later in the Bear Paw Mountains.

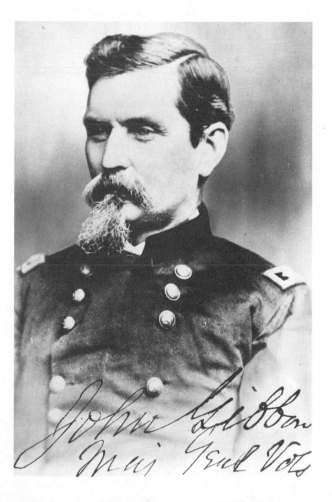

the soldiers were besieged for nearly 36 hours. Although the Nez Percé had been taken by surprise, they rallied and successfully evaded the army once again. But this time, the encounter broke their spirits. Their losses of men and goods, to say nothing of their personal family losses, and the realization that they would be pursued no matter where they went in the American West, left them without hope. Finally, in the evening of the second day of fighting (August 10), the warriors fired parting shots and left to join their people. The Battle of Big Hole was over.

big hole national battlefield

FEET 0   1500
METERS 0   500

FORT HARTSTUFF STATE HISTORICAL PARK

R.R., Burwell, NB 68823

Telephone: (308) 346-4715

Curator: Mr. Roye D. Lindsay

Hours: Daily, May through October

Cost of admission: Free to the public

Description: All nine original buildings of this 1870s Indian War Infantry post remain. Buildings are of grout (concretelike) construction and hence are much more well preserved than other forts of the 1870s. Restoration is nearly complete. All buildings are refurnished with period materials. The fort is significant in that it typifies the military/settler phase of federal presence on the frontier. It also protected friendly Indians (Pawnee) from the more hostile Sioux. It came into being as a result of conflict between the Indians (mostly Teton Sioux) and white settlers in the North Loop Valley, and was named for Maj. Gen. George L. Hartstuff, a Civil War hero. After the War between the States, home-

Troops in Civil War uniforms fire flag salute near Fort Hartstuff's 95-foot flagstaff on Memorial Day 1979. They are firing the newfangled .45-70 Springfield: the carbine, officer's model, and rifle. Barracks in background.

steaders streamed into the area, eager to stake their claims to free government land. They encroached on lands the Indians traditionally roamed at will. One skirmish between Indians and whites on Sioux Creek, 15 miles west of this site, resulted in a loss of $1,500 worth of horses, a huge sum in those days.

112

Aerial view of Fort Hartstuff, 1978. *Clockwise, lower left center:* post headquarters; guardhouse; laundress quarters (ruins); quartermaster's storehouse; stables (distance); hospital; commanding officer's quarters (ruins, in process of restoration); officers' quarters; barracks (restoration completed 1979).

Front parlor in officers' quarters.

FORT ROBINSON MUSEUM

State Historical Society Site, P. O. Box 304, Crawford, NB 69339

Telephone: (308) 665-2852

Curator: Vance E. Nelson

Hours: April 1 to November 15, Monday through Saturday 8 A.M. to 5 P.M.; Sunday 1 P.M. to 5 P.M.

Cost of admission: Free to the public

Description: Fort Robinson is 3 miles west of Crawford on U.S. 20. It is located in the Pine Ridge country near the Black Hills. At one time or another, it has served as home for soldiers, civilians, and Indians. The adobe officers' quarters is open to the public and is one of nearly 50 structures remaining at Fort Robinson. Other museum structures are the restored blacksmith, harness repair, and wheelwright shops. The veterinarian hospital and the 1905 post office still stand, as do the log guardhouse and adju-

tant's office (1874). The old parade grounds, site of the death of the great Sioux Chief Crazy Horse, are still intact. The museum proper is in the post headquarters building and displays many artifacts of the frontier struggle that took place on this site.

Fort Robinson Museum.

FORT ATKINSON STATE PARK MUSEUM

P. O. Box 237, Fort Calhoun, NB 68023
Telephone: (402) 468-5895
Curator and Park Director: Steve Kemper
Hours: Mid-May to early September 10 A.M. to 8 P.M., or by appointment
Cost of admission: Free to the public
Description: Fort Atkinson was established as a result of the Yellowstone Expedition of 1819, but its story begins 15 years before with the Lewis and Clark Expedition. Lewis and Clark camped in this area during the summer of 1804 and held council with the Otoe and other Indian tribes on August 3, 1804, naming the locale "Council Bluffs." It was then Clark recommended the site for a fort. In 1819 the Yellowstone Expedition was sent to establish a chain of outposts from the mouth of the Missouri River to the Yellowstone River. Fort Atkinson became the largest post in the West, with a garrison of over 1,000 men during its active period. Such a large garrison exerted a positive influence on the Indians and European traders. Among units stationed there were the elite Rifle Regiment and the famed "Fighting 6th" Infantry. The 2 units were later consolidated into one regiment.

Interior of parade ground at Fort Atkinson showing entrances to individual rooms (under reconstruction).

Colonial battleflag, musket, uniform, and artifacts.

FORT OMAHA MUSEUM

General Crook House, Fort Omaha, NB 68111
Telephone: (402) 455-9990
Director: Patricia Pixley
Hours: Thursday through Sunday noon to 3 P.M., or by appointment; closed holidays
Cost of admission: Adults $1; children 50¢
Description: Fort Omaha was established in 1868. Omaha's location on a natural route to the West made it a logical base from which to provide support for the troops engaged in the Indian Wars, as well as to protect the crew constructing the Union Pacific and the Northern Pacific railroads. World War I recruits trained at the fort, and the Army Balloon School was estab-

114

lished there to train aeronauts. During World War II the Signal Corps again made use of Fort Omaha as a training facility. The U.S. Navy took over the fort in 1948 and it was used as a Navy Reserve Command Post until 1973. Metropolitan Technical Community College purchased the fort in 1974 and it now serves as its Fort Omaha campus. Indian fighters, aeronauts, sailors, and now students have found a use for historic Fort Omaha. The General Crook House has been set aside as a museum to preserve the fort's past military history and record of historic frontier events.

An army supply convoy marches across open country.

FORT KEARNY STATE HISTORICAL PARK

Rt. 4, Kearny, NB 68847
Telephone: (308) 234-9513
Curator: Roger G. Sykes
Hours: Monday through Friday 10 A.M. to 8 P.M.
in season; weekends 8 A.M. to 8 P.M.
Cost of admission: Free to the public
Description: The visitor center contains artifacts from original site. A slide show on Fort Kearny lasts 15 minutes. Maps and information on fort and old buildings are available. In 1846 Col. Kearny with a detachment of troops proceeded up the Missouri from Fort Leavenworth and laid out the site of the fort and made arrangements for its construction. A 2-story blockhouse was completed before the army realized that the location was ill-chosen for its purpose, because at that date very few emigrants passed that point. The name Camp Kearny was first applied to the post, but later it was called Fort Kearny.

The museum building at Fort Kearny. Note sod roof.

STATE ARSENAL MUSEUM

17th and Court sts., Lincoln, NB 68508
Telephone: (402) 473-1151
Curator: Lt. Col. Laurence G. Lade (Ret.)
Hours: Irregular
Cost of admission: Not determined
Description: This is a new museum housing military artifacts, particularly those applicable to the Nebraska National Guard, including uniform items from post–Civil War to present and a limited outdoor display of military vehicles. Its library houses old Nebraska National Guard records and many outdated technical publications. The museum building itself is historically significant as the first structure built by the State of Nebraska for use of the Nebraska National Guard.

State Arsenal Museum, Lincoln.

FORT CHURCHILL HISTORICAL STATE MONUMENT

Silver Springs, NV 89429
Telephone: (702) 577-2345
Director: Superintendent, Nevada Division of State Parks
Hours: Daily 8 A.M. to 5 P.M.

Cost of admission: Free to the public
Description: Artifacts on display date from the 1860s when the fort was active; board displays with drawings depict this area's history. In the center of the museum room is a model of the original fort, and the museum is built of the same material. Several 3-inch Army Ordnance rifles are on display outside the museum building; these are original cannons that have been restored.

ARRADCOM MUSEUM

Picatinny Arsenal, Dover, NJ 07801
Telephone: (201) 328-2797
Curator: Thomas C. Cavanaugh
Hours: Tuesday through Friday 9 A.M. to 3 P.M.
Cost of admission: Free to the public
Description: The museum collection has over 9,000 items, including Civil War ammunition, German ammunition (Franco-Prussian War through World War II), U.S. ammunition and fuses; subcollections of British, French, Russian, Red Chinese, Japanese, Italian, and Belgian

Weapons, ammunition, and military accouterments are on wide display at the Arradcom Museum.

items (mainly battlefield recovery sent to Picatinny Arsenal for technical study); manuscripts and handwritten ledgers of the early days of the arsenal (1879–1904) and reports of the Chief of Ordnance (1879–1920).

For historians with an explosive bent, this array of early American ammunition is the most complete in the country.

COMMUNICATIONS-ELECTRONICS MUSEUM

Fort Monmouth, NJ 07703
Telephone: (201) 532-2445
Curator: Edmond J. Norris
Hours: Monday through Friday 8 A.M. to 4 P.M.; closed holidays
Cost of admission: Free to the public
Description: In the years of our nation's birth and early development, in war and in peace, communications opened the frontiers for the New World. However, it was not until 1860, when the U.S. Army Signal Corps was founded, that the science of modern communications was presented for the world to emulate. Throughout its history, the exploits of the Signal Corps, its heritage and accomplishments, have placed it at the fore of the world's communicators. Its successor, the U.S. Army Electronics Command, one of the greatest technological centers in the world, carries on the proud tradition. The museum is a military wonderworld. It displays uniforms from 1860 to the present; Civil War equipment; air-to-ground communications systems; the story of the laser; pigeons of fame; solar cells, fuel cells, batteries, and cameras.

Entrance to Communications—Electronics Museum at Fort Monmouth.

Displays of uniforms from 1860 to the present.

In this electronic museum there is a world of military gadgetry to be seen, heard, and inspected.

Tactical radios: two decades of miniaturization.

MORRISTOWN NATIONAL HISTORIC PARK

P.O. Box 1136R, 230 Morris Ave. W., Morristown, NJ 07960

Telephone: (201) 539-2016

Superintendent: William G. Binnewies

Hours: Daily 9 A.M. to 5 P.M.; closed Thanksgiving, Christmas, and New Year's Day

Cost of admission: Adults 50¢

Description: Morristown headquarters museum tells the story of an army struggling to survive. During two critical winters, the town sheltered the main encampment of the Continental Army. In 1777 George Washington overcame desertion, hunger, and disease to rebuild an army capable of taking the field against William Howe's veteran Redcoats. In 1779–80 (the hardest winter in anyone's memory) the military

Diorama of Washington on the steps of the Ford Mansion, which served as his headquarters while in Morristown, N.J. (1779–80), greeting Lafayette.

Morristown National Historical Park in New Jersey is the site of important military encampments during the Revolutionary War, and now a leading National Park Service site visited by thousands annually. Morristown served as Washington's headquarters in 1777 and 1779–80.

struggle was almost lost amid starvation, nakedness, and mutiny on the bleak hills of Jockey Hollow. Never was the leadership of Washington more evident as he held together, at a desperate time, the small ragged army that represented this country's main hope to independence. Morristown includes a refurbished Ford Mansion (Washington's headquarters) built in 1774; the Wick farmhouse built in 1750 (also refurbished); the headquarters museum; and Jockey Hollow Visitor Center, which also houses exhibits relating to the Revolutionary War.

OLD BARRACKS MUSEUM

S. Willow St., Trenton, NJ 08608
Telephone: (609) 396-1776
Curator: Cynthia Koch
Hours: Daily, April through October 10 A.M. to 5 P.M.; November through March 10 A.M. to 4:30 P.M.; closed Thanksgiving, Christmas Eve, Christmas, and New Year's Day
Cost of admission: Adults 50¢; children to 12 years, 25¢; school groups, senior citizens, and special groups free
Description: The Old Barracks, built in 1758, is a handsome fieldstone structure built during the French and Indian War, to prevent the forcible billeting of British soldiers with private householders. The situation had become so intolerable in the winters, when troops were withdrawn from the frontiers to the towns, that petitions by citizens were sent to the General Assembly of the province of New Jersey for "adequate remedy." The General Assembly replied by erecting five barracks for winter quarters for 1,500

Old Barracks Museum, Trenton, N.J.

men. The Trenton Barracks is the only one that survives. As a museum, it displays a large collection of period firearms, accouterments, and uniforms; restored soldiers' quarters; a diorama of the Battle of Trenton; furniture, silver, and china of colonial period, and other memorabilia.

BILLY THE KID MUSEUM

Rt. 1, Box 36, Fort Sumner, NM 88119
Telephone: (505) 355-2380
Director: Don Sweet
Hours: March through December, Monday through Saturday; closed Thanksgiving and Christmas
Admission: Adults (12 years and over) $1.50; children (6 to 11 years) 75¢, under 6 years free

Description: The general museum houses 60,000 items pertaining to the frontier days of Billy the Kid, Kit Carson, Geronimo, Pat Garrett, and the U.S. Cavalry. Its collection includes items used in the old fort, Indian artifacts, and some antique cars and pieces of ancient farm machinery. Located at the east end of Fort Sumner on U.S. 60, the museum offers ample free parking.

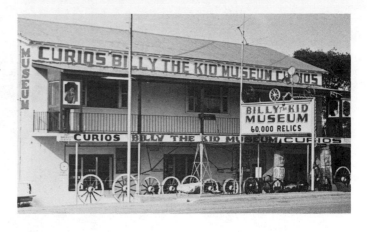
Billy the Kid Museum, Fort Sumner.

FORT SELDEN STATE MONUMENT

P.O. Box 58, Radium Springs, NM 88054
Telephone: (505) 526-8911
Curator: Rudy Saucedo
Hours: Thursday through Monday 9 A.M. to 5 P.M.
Cost of admission: Free to the public

Description: On display are artifacts excavated at Fort Selden, including items from the Indian Wars, period uniforms, 3-inch ordnance rifle model 1865, and photographs of the original fort and of the McArthur family, who were at Fort Selden from 1884 to 1886. A self-guided trail makes it possible for a visitor to see both the old and new of the fort.

FORT UNION NATIONAL MONUMENT

Watrous, NM 87753
Telephone: (505) 425-8025 or 454-1155
Chief Ranger: Lalo Navarrete
Hours: Daily 8 A.M. to 4:30 P.M.; closed Christmas and New Year's Day
Cost of admission: Free to the public

Description: Fort Union is 8 miles north of I-25, at the end of N.Mex. 477. Watrous is ½ mile south of the intersection of these 2 highways. The nearest large community is Las Vegas, N. Mex., which is 26 miles south. The museum depicts life and activities during the founding, building, and use of Fort Union from 1851 to 1891. It shows how the Santa Fe Trail affected the development of the Southwest. Displays include: land ownership (Spanish, Mexican, and United States); the location and founding of Fort Union; the three forts; the enlisted soldier; the cavalry; the infantry; garrison life; weapons of the west; the Indian Wars; Fort Union and the Civil War; the military supply function of Fort Union; early transportation on the Santa Fe Trail; and artillery in the West. Also in the museum is a scale model of the third Fort Union and a 12-pound mountain howitzer.

In a demonstration of living history, a gun crew prepares a Parrott 10-pounder for firing. This was a popular field piece in the post–Civil War years.

121

Many of the original buildings still stand at Fort Union. They are gradually being restored to their original appearance.

CROWN POINT STATE HISTORIC SITE

R.D. 1, Box 219, Crown Point, NY 12928
Telephone: (518) 597-3666
Historic Site Manager: Gregory T. Furness
Hours: Memorial Day weekend to October 15,
Tuesday through Sunday 9 A.M. to 5 P.M.; or by
appointment
Cost of admission: Free to the public

Description: The 2 major exhibits at the site are the carefully preserved original ruins of Fort St. Frederic constructed by the French (1734–37), and Fort Crown Point constructed by the British (1759–63). These had been built to control the strategic inland route between Montreal and Albany formed by Lake Champlain. A visitor center building houses changing exhibits on the history and archeology of Crown Point, and an introductory audiovisual program on the site. Research files are maintained and are open to the public by appointment. Exhibits deal with

Fort Crown Point soldiers' barracks.

the American, British, and French military occupations in the period from 1730 to 1780. In 1759, there were 2,620 Massachusetts men, 694 Rhode Island men, 3,640 Connecticut men, and 928 New York men at work on the immense new structure.

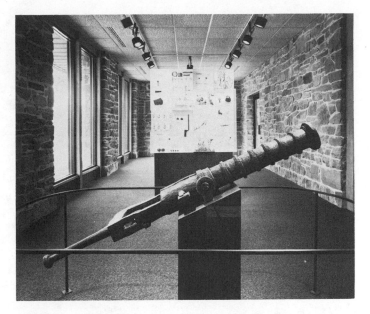

Seventeenth-century breech-loaded swivel cannon excavated from the ruins of Fort St. Frederic.

REMINGTON GUN MUSEUM

Remington Arms Company, Ilion, NY 13357
Telephone: (315) 894-9961
Curator: Laurence K. Goodstal
Hours: Monday through Saturday 9 A.M. to 5 P.M.;
Sunday 1 P.M. to 5 P.M.
Cost of admission: Free to the public

Description: On display are Remington firearms from the first flintlock and percussion types of 1816–1850, through cartridge models from early Rolling Block (1864), to contemporary rifles and shotguns.

The new Remington Gun Museum.

The first Remington gun, a flintlock rifle, was made here in 1816.

Revolvers *(left to right):* Beals, Army; Model 1861, Army;
and New Model, Army.

High grade handguns *(top to bottom):* Model 1875, Army;
New Model packet; Navy (.36-cal.) Transformed Model;
New Model No. 4; Model 1890 No. 4.

WASHINGTON'S HEADQUARTERS STATE HISTORIC SITE

84 Liberty St., Newburgh, NY 12550

Telephone: (914) 562-1195

Hours: Wednesday through Sunday 9 A.M. to 5 P.M.

Cost of admission: Free to the public

Description: To reach the site, take Thruway 17 (Newburgh), then go left on 17K into Newburgh. This fieldstone home of Jonathan Hasbrouck overlooking the Hudson River at Newburgh served as George Washington's headquarters between April 1782 and August 1783. While he awaited the peace treaty with Great Britain, Washington countered the political maneuvers and growing discontent of his officers. Extensive exhibits and an audiovisual program are located in an adjacent museum building. Within its parklike setting, the little-altered Hasbrouck House still stands vigil over the Hudson River landscape.

Hasbrouck House, last headquarters of Washington during the Revolution, part of Washington's Headquarters State Historic Site.

Section of exhibit at the museum, showing weapons used by the Americans during the Revolutionary War.

HARBOR DEFENSE MUSEUM OF NEW YORK CITY

Fort Hamilton, Brooklyn, NY 11252
Telephone: (212) 836-4100 or 836-4149
Director: Russell S. Gilmore, Ph.D.
Hours: Monday through Friday 1 P.M. to 4 P.M.;
Saturdays 10 A.M. to 5 P.M.; Sunday 1 P.M. to 5
P.M.; Closed for 10 days during Christmas season
Cost of admission: Free to the public
Description: The Harbor Defense Museum replaces the Fort Wadsworth Museum as the U.S. Army Museum in New York City. The museum displays weapons, uniforms, documents, paintings, posters, and other memorabilia related to the history of New York City. Its collection includes medals, models, and artillery.

Rodman gun in John Paul Jones Park, just outside Fort Hamilton in Brooklyn. One of only two 20-inch Rodmans made. Tested at Fort Hamilton in 1864.

CASTLE CLINTON NATIONAL MONUMENT

Address inquiries to: Nat'l Park Service, 26 Wall St., New York, NY 10005
Telephone: (212) 344-7220
Superintendent: Duane Pearson
Hours: Daily 9 A.M. to 4:30 P.M.; closed Thanksgiving, Christmas, and New Year's Day
Cost of admission: Free to the public
Description: Located at the tip of Manhattan, the museum has restored officers' quarters, artifacts, and photos of the fort's 4 phases. Circular in shape, the southwest battery once stood in

Castle Clinton.

128

about 35 feet of water, 200 feet from shore. A timber causeway with drawbridge connected the new fort to Manhattan. The southwest battery had 28 guns on one tier. Inside the rounded ends of the rear wall, on the land side, were the magazines. Quarters for the officers were at each side of the passageway to the causeway. No barracks for the enlisted men existed. The southwest battery was completed in 1811 and fired its first salute on November 25, the twenty-eighth anniversary of the departure of the British from New York at the close of the American Revolution. Throughout the War of 1812 the fort stood ready, but its guns fired at nothing more dangerous than a harmless hulk moored in the river for target practice.

FORT ONTARIO STATE HISTORIC SITE

Oswego, NY 13126

Telephone: (315) 343-4711

Cost of admission: Nominal fee Memorial Day to Labor Day

Description: The site is located three blocks north of Rt. 104 (E. Bridge St.) at foot of E. 7th St. Great Britain, France, and finally the United States struggled to control Fort Ontario. From the time of the French and Indian War until a peaceful frontier with Canada was achieved, this

Members of the Fort Ontario Guard, a re-created Civil War artillery unit.

Exterior view of Fort Ontario State Historic Site, showing sally port and two bastions.

strategic fortress commanded the route from the Hudson and Mohawk valleys to the Great Lakes. Today visitors peer through the gunports in great stone walls, examine the guardhouse and the powder magazine, and step into an officer's home. Exhibits explain how the fort was constructed and why.

Inside the walls of Fort Ontario, showing a Civil War era twelve-pounder Napoleon.

FORT STANWIX NATIONAL MONUMENT

Address inquiries to: Nat'l Park Service, 112 E. Park St., Rome, NY 13440
Telephone: (315) 336-2090
Superintendent: Lee Hanson
Hours: Monday through Friday 9 A.M. to 5 P.M.; weekends 9 A.M. to 6 P.M.; closed Labor Day and Christmas

Cost of admission: Free to the public

Description: Fort Stanwix is a reconstruction of an 18th-century fort in a 15-acre park setting with furnished barracks and officers' quarters. Costumed interpreters explain life in a military outpost during the Revolution. There is also a film on the siege of Fort Stanwix in 1777 and a display of 18th-century artifacts found on the site by archeologists prior to reconstruction. Public restrooms are available and the park is accessible to the handicapped. Parking is 1 block from the fort entrance.

Model for reconstruction of Fort Stanwix.

Actors in authentic uniforms play out the exciting history of Fort Stanwix.

A member of the garrison examines Oneida Indian crafts at Fort Stanwix.

ORISKANY BATTLEFIELD STATE HISTORIC SITE

Rt. 69 between Rome and Utica, NY

Telephone: (315) 768-7224

Hours: Mid-April to mid-October 9 A.M. to 5 P.M.;

Sunday 1 P.M. to 5 P.M.; closed Tuesdays

Cost of admission: Free to the public

Description: From Thruway exit 32 (Westmoreland), take Rt. 233 to Rt. 69. to reach the site. On August 6, 1777, the rebel militia of the upper Mohawk Valley and the forces of the British Crown met in fierce hand-to-hand combat at the place known ever since as Oriskany Battlefield. The battle served as a discouraging blow to an invading British army besieging nearby Fort Stanwix and thus helped to turn the course of the Revolution. "Oriskany Day" early in August commemorates the battle's anniversary. Picnic grounds are available, and on Wednesday, Thursday, and Friday evenings through July and early August there is a free film festival.

At Oriskany Battlefield State Historic Site, a Metalphoto sign explains the course of the battle after the British ambushed the Americans.

Monument at Oriskany Battlefield State Historic Site.

SACKETS HARBOR BATTLEFIELD STATE HISTORIC SITE

Sackets Harbor, NY 13685

Telephone: (315) 646-3634

Hours: Memorial Day weekend to Labor Day,
Tuesday through Saturday 9 A.M. to 5 P.M.; Sunday
1 P.M. to 5 P.M.

Cost of admission: Free to the public

Description: The site is located on the west side of Sackets Harbor Village, 1 mile from Rt. 3, and 8 miles from Exit 45 of I-81. During the War of 1812, Sackets Harbor, a small American port on Lake Ontario, became an important military and naval base. With abundant supply of nearby timber, the Americans built ships here to oppose the British and Canadians. Following an American raid on New York (now Toronto), the British raided Sackets Harbor in May of 1813.

New York State militia cavalry officer's coat, and reproduction 1813 leather cap worn by Corps of Artillery, on display at the Union Hotel visitors center.

Commandant's and lieutenants' houses, 1848, at Sackets Harbor Battlefield State Historic Site. The small reproduction naval cannon in the foreground is used for demonstrations by a re-created 1812 gun crew.

SARATOGA NATIONAL HISTORICAL PARK VISITOR CENTER AND MUSEUM

R.D. 1, Stillwater, NY 12170

Telephone: (518) 664-9821

Superintendent: W. Glen Gray

Hours: Daily 9 A.M. to 5 P.M.; closed Thanksgiving, Christmas, and New Year's Day

Cost of admission: Free to the public

Description: Saratoga National Historical Park is the site of the battles of Saratoga which occurred on September 19, 1777, and October 7, 1777. These sites are located in the township of Stillwater, N.Y., in between the present communities of Schuylerville and Stillwater. The park entrances lie 30 miles north of Albany, N.Y., on

One of the original garrison guns still showing the royal British seal.

British troops lined up on the field of combat as they were on the day the Battle of Saratoga began.

U.S. 4, and N.Y. 32. At this facility a 21-minute color motion picture entitled *Checkmate on the Hudson* can be seen. This film uses a *Kriegspiel* technique, utilizing military miniatures to portray the battles, and features Burgess Meredith as a neutral narrator. There are exhibits highlighting some of the artifacts of the battles and the period.

Benedict Arnold's headquarters.

The new wing of the visitors center at Saratoga.

STONY POINT STATE HISTORIC SITE

P.O. Box 182, Stony Point, NY 10980
Telephone: (914) 786-2521
Hours: Mid-April through October, Wednesday through Sunday 9 A.M. to 5 P.M.
Cost of admission: Free to the public
Description: The site is east off Rt. 9W, just north of community of Stony Point. On July 16, 1779, Gen. Anthony Wayne led a daring midnight raid of American Light Infantrymen against the British-held positions at Stony Point. Americans won a stunning victory. They carried the grudging respect of their enemy, and ended the last serious British attempts to draw out and crush Washington's forces in the north. At Stony Point Museum you can see sights and sounds of the battle through exhibits and an audiovisual program. On the summit of the Stony Point peninsula stands an 1826 fieldstone lighthouse that guided Hudson River traffic for 100 years.

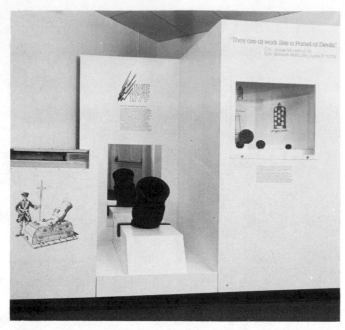

"Royal" 8-inch mortar, dated 1759, captured by the Americans at the Battle of Stony Point.

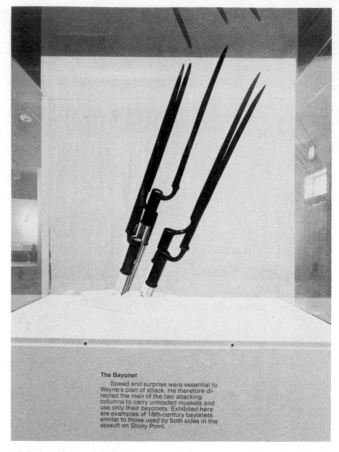

The Bayonet

Speed and surprise were essential to Wayne's plan of attack. He therefore directed the men of the two attacking columns to carry unloaded muskets and use only their bayonets. Exhibited here are examples of 18th-century bayonets similar to those used by both sides in the assault on Stony Point.

Eighteenth-century bayonets of the type used at the Battle of Stony Point, displayed at Stony Point Battlefield State Historic Site.

FORT MOUNT HOPE

Burgoyne Road, Ticonderoga, NY 12883
Telephone: (518) 585-4477
Director and Curator: Carroll V. Lonergan
Hours: Daily, May 25 to October 15 9 A.M. to
5 P.M.

Cost of admission: Donations only

Description: Fort Mount Hope is located high on a hill overlooking Lake Champlain and the valley of Ticonderoga. The setting is delightful; nothing modern detracts from the antiquity and quiet solitude on a warm summer afternoon or a crisp October morning. Here you may slip easily into the hallowed past and roam the old breastworks again with Burgoyne's men, or Rogers' Rangers, or Brown's colonials. Fort Mount Hope is a truly romantic spot.

NEW WINDSOR CANTONMENT STATE HISTORIC SITE

Temple Hill Rd., P.O. Box 207, Vails Gate, NY 12584
Telephone: (914) 561-1765
Curator: Howard Miller
Hours: Wednesday through Sunday 9 A.M. to 5 P.M.
Cost of admission: Free to the public
Description: The story of the Continental Army's last winter encampment is portrayed through a variety of original and reconstructed buildings, museum exhibits, and demonstrations. Special programs and weekend events depict the daily life-style of the common soldier during the American Revolution. Such programs include 18th-century military encampments, military shows, musical reviews, and displays of various 18th-century crafts. A military village of some 700 buildings, the New Windsor Cantonment, housed 6,000–8,000 soldiers during its 8 months of use. This was a period of great uncertainty and tribulation for the soldiers. Peace negotiations were proceeding slowly. While the Continental Congress debated policy, back pay was piling up, inflation was rampant, and discontent was growing. Resentment spread among the officers. Washington's character and statesmanship broke the budding mutiny.

Revolutionary War 6-pounder cannon on reproduction carriages.

This wooden structure was built by Revolutionary soldiers in 1782 at the New Windsor Cantonment and is the only one of its kind to survive to the 20th century.

WEST POINT MUSEUM

U.S. Military Academy, West Point, NY 10996
Telephone: (914) 938-3201, 938-3100, or
938-2203
Director: Richard E. Kuehne
Hours: Daily 10:30 A.M. to 4:15 P.M.; closed
Christmas and New Year's Day
Cost of admission: Free to the public

Description: Collection includes nearly 20,000 arms, both European and American, pole arms, guns, cannon, flags, uniforms, prints, drawings, and distinctive collection of paintings related to the history of military science both European and American. Paintings are internationally known and dating to the mid-18th century. Collection noted for West Point–related artifacts including portraits, cadet uniforms, artifacts, and personal memorabilia.

A view of the collection at the West Point Museum.

Bicentennial display: America and Allies, Revolutionary War.

OLD FORT NIAGARA

P.O. Box 169, Youngstown, NY 14174
Telephone: (716) 745-7611
Director: Brian Leigh Dunnigan
Hours: Daily 9 A.M. to dusk; closed Thanksgiving,
Christmas, and New Year's Day
Cost of admission: Adults $2; children 50¢

Description: The fort's six original 18th-century buildings date from 1726 to 1771. On display are 18th-century fortification walls, archeological exhibits, and a large collection of firearms and artillery. The oldest, largest, and most important of the pre-Revolutionary buildings of Old Fort Niagara was designed and built by King Louis XV's chief engineer in Canada, during the year of 1726. The Indians were

Two of the original buildings of Old Fort Niagara. On the left is the blockhouse constructed by the British in 1762. The larger building is the "Castle." This structure was erected by the French in 1726 as part of the first Niagara.

deceived into believing it was to be merely a "stone house for trading," for, as they greatly outnumbered the whites, their permission for its erection was felt necessary. However, the "stone house" turned out to be one of the most strongly fortified buildings in America.

MOORES CREEK NATIONAL BATTLEFIELD

P.O. Box 69, Currie, NC 28435
Telephone: (919) 283-5591
Superintendent: John W. Stockert
Hours: Daily 8 A.M. to 5 P.M.; closed Christmas and New Year's Day
Cost of admission: Free to the public
Description: The site offers a narrated slide presentation, informational exhibits and panels, a diorama, 18th-century artifacts, a Brown Bess musket, a Scots Highland pistol, a fowling piece, a broadsword, and a bronze ½-pounder swivel

Visitor center, Moores Creek National Battlefield.

gun. At Moores Creek Bridge, in a brief but violent clash in the morning darkness of February 27, 1776, North Carolina patriots defeated a larger Loyalist force of Scots and Crown sympathizers on its way to meet with a British expeditionary squadron on the coast. Small as the battle was, the victory ended forever royal authority in the colony, helped forestall a full-scale invasion of the South, and encouraged North Carolina on April 12, 1776, to instruct its delegation to the Continental Congress in Philadelphia to vote for independence—the first colony to do so.

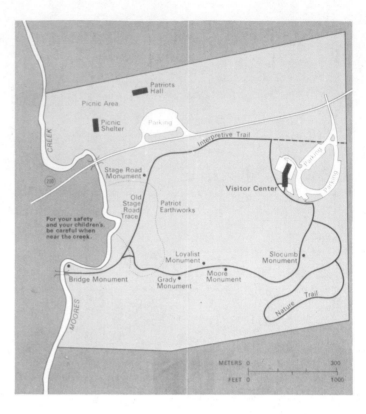

GUILFORD COURTHOUSE NATIONAL MILITARY PARK

P.O. Box 9806, Greensboro, NC 27408
Telephone: (919) 288-1776
Superintendent: W. W. Danielson
Hours: Daily 8:30 A.M. to 5 P.M., extended during summer; closed Christmas and New Year's Day
Cost of admission: Free to the public
Description: Guilford Courthouse National Military Park is located 6 miles north of downtown Greensboro, N.C., off U.S. 220 on New Garden Rd. Museum exhibits focus on March 15, 1781, Battle of Guilford Courthouse. Exhibits include weapons of the Revolution along with equipment displayed on mannequins representing soldiers of both sides. A special exhibit with personal effects honors Peter Francisco. Cases exhibit artifacts recovered from the battlefield. Visual displays focus on battle leaders. Self-start film demonstrates loading and firing of musket,

Visitor center houses an auditorium and museum exhibits.

140

rifle, and cannon. Campaign and battle maps are also shown. On March 15, 1781, an American army commanded by Gen. Nathanael Greene made its stand at Guilford Courthouse to contest the invasion of North Carolina by the British forces of Lord Charles Cornwallis.

The most impressive of the exhibits is this mannequin display using actual arms and equipment of the Revolutionary period.

KINGS MOUNTAIN NATIONAL MILITARY PARK

P.O. Box 31, Kings Mountain, NC 28086
Telephone: (803) 936-7508 or 936-7472
Superintendent: Andrew M. Loveless
Hours: Daily 9 A.M. to 5 P.M.; closed Christmas
Cost of admission: Free to the public

Description: Kings Mountain is easily reached from Charlotte, N.C., by I-85; from Spartanburg, S.C., by I-85; and from York, S.C., by S.C. 161. The visitor center museum displays 18th-century tools, weapons, furniture, clothing, and artifacts. It was here that a ragtag American army, called "over-mountain men," fought a bloody but victorious battle that ultimately delayed British Gen. Charles Cornwallis's plans for 3 months. During this time the Continental Army organized a new offensive in the South. At Charlotte, in December 1780, Gen. Nathanael Greene replaced Gen. Horatio Gates as Continental Army Commander of the Southern Department and seized from Cornwallis the military initiative in the Carolinas. The British general never regained the initiative and ul-

Kings Mountain National Military Park, where American frontiersmen won an important victory in 1780.

timately was forced to surrender at Yorktown in Virginia. Kings Mountain thus became Cornwallis's first misstep toward his defeat that marked the end of a long and bitter war.

Visitors view monument at Kings Mountain.

FORT FISHER STATE HISTORIC SITE

Hwy. 421 South, Kure Beach, N.C.

Address inquiries to: P.O. Box 68, Kure Beach, NC 28449

Telephone: (919) 458-5538

Manager: E. Gehrig Spencer

Hours: Tuesday through Sunday 9 A.M. to 5 P.M.; closed Thanksgiving and Christmas

Cost of admission: Free to the public

Description: The museum offers 15-minute slide orientation program, a 6-minute movie on the fall of Fort Fisher, artifacts, Civil War relics, a self-guided tour of the museum and earthworks, plus numerous other sightseeing features. The state operates a laboratory at Fort Fisher for the preservation of underwater treasures. There are thought to be as many as 50 sunken Civil War ships in the coastal waters of the Wilmington area—many of them unexplored. Fort Fisher was named in honor of Col. Charles F. Fisher. It was the largest Civil War earthwork fortification in the Confederacy. On April 24, 1861, Confederate Point (now Federal Point) was taken over by the Confederates, and sand batteries mounting 17 guns constructed. Later, a new and powerful Fort Fisher, mounting 47 heavy guns was constructed. The heaviest naval bombardments up to that time took place there on December 24–25, 1864, and January 13–15, 1865, when the fort fell to the Union forces.

Visitor center/museum, with plenty of parking space, at Fort Fisher State Historic Site.

The museum gives a lucid explanation of the defenses at Fort Fisher.

FORT RALEIGH NATIONAL HISTORIC SITE, LINDSAY WARREN VISITOR CENTER

Rt. 1, Box 675, Manteo, NC 27954
Telephone: (919) 473-5772

Superintendent: William A. Harris; Curator: James Eldridge
Hours: Daily 8 A.M. to 5 P.M.
Cost of admission: Free to the public
Description: Fort Raleigh is part of the "Outer Banks" National Seashore complex. At the visitor center are exhibit cases and panels presenting 16th-century ship models, early navigational aids, military equipment, ancient helmets,

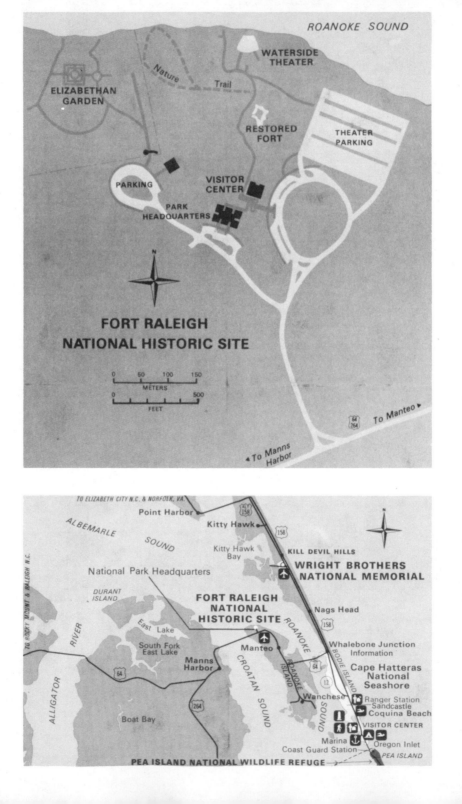

breastplates, halberds, matchlock muskets, dioramas, artifacts, and 16th-century breechloading swivel guns. This site commemorates the Lost Colony, which was one of several unsuccessful attempts by Sir Walter Raleigh to settle Roanoke Island in the 1580s. Farther south, at Coquin Beach, a small museum displays equipment used by the U.S. Life-Saving Service.

FORT ABERCROMBIE STATE HISTORIC SITE

Abercrombie, ND 58001
Telephone: (701) 553-8513 or 553-8719
Curator: Mrs. Susan Forness
Hours: May through September, Monday through Saturday 8 A.M. to 6 P.M.; Sunday 10 A.M. to 6 years P.M.
Cost of admission: Adults 50¢; children (6 years and over) 25¢

Description: Fort Abercrombie was established on August 28, 1858, by Lt. Col. John J. Abercrombie, U.S. Army. Fort Abercrombie was built on the west bank of the Red River of the North at the approximate head of navigation. This post protected the northwestern frontier and became a link in a chain of military posts extending along the route from St. Paul to the Montana gold fields. It also guarded the traffic along the Red River to Canada. A modern building houses the military museum.

Fort Abercrombie State Historic Site Museum.

Fort Abercrombie stage.

CAMP HANCOCK STATE HISTORIC SITE

1st and Main sts., Bismarck, ND 58501
Telephone: (701) 224-2465
Site Supervisor: F. J. Giedt
Hours: Hours vary

Cost of admission: Free to the public
Description: Camp Hancock, now a state-owned site, preserves part of a military camp established to provide protection for work gangs building part of the Northern Pacific Railroad. A log headquarters building (now wood-sheathed) still stands on the site and is used as an interpretive center and museum.

FORT TOTTEN STATE HISTORIC SITE

Fort Totten, ND 58335
Telephone: (701) 766-4441
Site Supervisor: George Grove
Hours: Daily 8 A.M. to 8 P.M.
Cost of admission: Free to the public
Description: Said to be the best preserved military post of the Indian War period, Fort Totten has a military museum maintained by the Lake Region Pioneer Daughters. An interpretive center, designed and maintained by the State Historical Society of North Dakota, has just recently opened its doors. The original fort was established by Gen. Alfred H. Terry on the south shore of Devils Lake on July 17, 1867. Named in honor of Maj. Gen. Joseph G. Totten, late chief of the Engineers, U.S. Army, it was built as part of a plan to place the Sisseton and Wahpeton Sioux on a reservation and as one of the posts to protect the overland route from southern Minnesota to western Montana.

The new Interpretive Center (museum) building recently opened to the public at Fort Totten. Formerly a commissary storehouse, it is one of the many original buildings belonging to the fort.

WHITESTONE HILL BATTLEFIELD STATE MUSEUM

Kulm, ND 58456
Telephone: (701) 396-7731
Site Supervisor: Eugene Orion
Hours: Daily, May 15 through September 30 8 A.M. to 8 P.M.
Cost of admission: Free to the public
Description: One of the most significant encounters between the whites and the Indians resulting from the Sioux uprising in Minnesota, the Battle of Whitestone Hill marked the beginning of a long war with the Plains Sioux, which was not to end until over 2 decades later. Owned by the State Historical Society, the museum houses many artifacts from the battle.

The monument in memory of the Minnesota militiamen who fell in combat at the Battle of Whitestone Hill.

FORT LINCOLN STATE PARK INTERPRETIVE CENTER

Fort Lincoln State Park, Rt. 2, Box 139, Mandan, ND 58554
Telephone: (701) 663-3049
Superintendent: Chuck Erickson
Hours: Daily, June, July, and August 8 A.M. to 9 P.M.; May, September 8 A.M. to 5 P.M.; October through April, Monday through Friday 8 A.M. to 5 P.M.
Cost of admission: Free to the public
Description: Located approximately 5 miles south of Mandan, N.D., the cavalry post was built in 1873. It became the headquarters of Lt. Col.

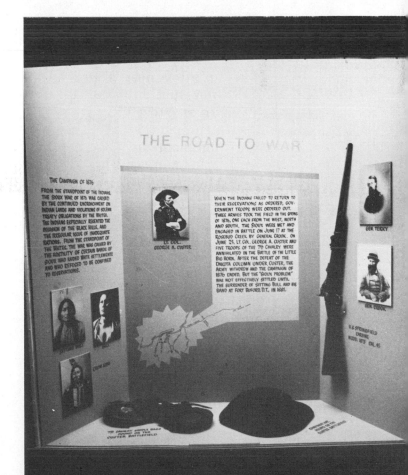

The Interpretive Center (museum) at Fort Lincoln contains many showcases honoring the memory of Lt. Col. Custer and the Battle of the Little Bighorn.

George Custer and the 7th Cavalry. In its heyday, the post, consisting of 655 officers and enlisted men, was occupied by 6 companies of the 7th Cavalry and 3 companies of the 6th and 17th Infantry. It was from Fort Lincoln that the 7th Cavalry under Custer rode out on the ill-fated campaign against the Plains Indians. This expedition culminated in the deaths of 265 men at the Battle of the Little Bighorn in Montana.

FORT PEMBINA STATE HISTORIC MUSEUM

Pembina, ND 58271
Telephone: (701) 825-6817
Curator: Mrs. Katheryn Grube
Cost of admission: Free to the public

Description: Fort Pembina, located near the confluence of the Red and Pembina rivers in Pembina County, commemorates the very beginning of recorded North Dakota history. The site has served many functions through the years including military and trading post, custom office, and post office. An on-site military museum interprets the history of the fort and the area. The property is state-owned.

The military museum building at Fort Pembina is convenient to the road and to public parking.

FORT BUFORD STATE HISTORIC SITE

Buford Rt., Williston, ND 58801
Telephone: (701) 572-9034
Site Supervisor: E. J. Duffey
Hours: Daily, May through September 8 A.M. to 5 P.M.; October through April by appointment only
Cost of admission: Adults 50¢; children (6 years and over) 25¢
Description: The U.S. Army established Fort

Buford near the confluence of the Missouri and Yellowstone rivers on June 13, 1866, as a link in the chain of "Missouri Guardian" posts reaching from the Mississippi River to the Pacific coast and intended it to defend the Missouri River and the Minnesota-Montana Road. Although protected by a 12-foot high stockade from 1867 to 1871, the fort suffered frequent harassment from Sioux Indians during its early years and recorded many hostile actions against the soldiers. The State Historical Society maintains a museum at the fort.

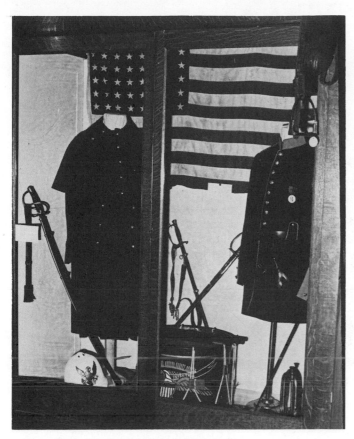

Fort Buford State Historic Site Museum.

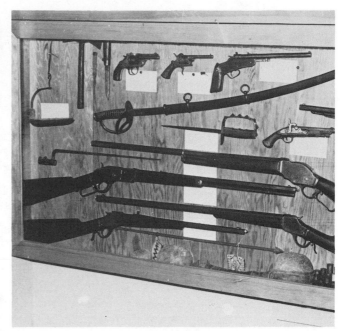

Weapons on display at Fort Buford.

FORT UNION NATIONAL HISTORIC SITE

Buford Rt., Williston, ND 58801
Telephone: (701) 572-9083
Area Manager: Bill Wellman
Hours: Daily 9 A.M. to 8 P.M.
Cost of admission: Free to the public
Description: This national historic site can be reached via Williston, N.D., which is 25 miles southwest via U.S. 2 and County Road 4. The fort was primarily a fur trading post, but also served as a military fort. The National Park Service owns Fort Union and maintains a military museum on the site.

Originally a trading post, later turned into a military outpost, Fort Union museum offers both Indian and military artifacts.

Lithograph of the first detailed sketch of Fort Union was drawn in 1833 by Karl Bodmer.

FORT LAURENS STATE MEMORIAL

Rt. 1, Bolivar, OH 44612

Telephone: (216) 874-2059

Area Manager: William McNealy; District Manager: Francis McMasters

Hours: Vary according to seasons of year. Closed Mondays

Cost of admission: Adults 75¢; children (6 to 12 years) 35¢

Description: Fort Laurens Museum exhibits many artifacts unearthed at the fort site in the summers of 1972 and 1973 during archeological explorations by the Ohio Historical Society. The museum also features costumed mannequins dressed in the uniforms of the soldiers and militiamen who built the fort, as well as weapons and accouterments of the American Revolution. Unifying the theme of the museum is a multiple-screen audiovisual program describing the history and background of the War for Independence and the Fort Laurens campaign.

FRANKLIN AREA HISTORICAL SOCIETY

302 Park Ave., Franklin, OH 45005
Telephone: (513) 746-8295
Curator: Mrs. Fred Reed
Hours: April through December, Sunday 3 P.M. to 5 P.M. or by appointment
Cost of admission: Adults 50¢; children 25¢
Description: The Gen. Forrest Harding Memorial Museum is located in the beautiful Harding home. The home, with most of its furnishings, was the gift of General and Mrs. Harding. Maj. Gen. E. F. Harding was born in Franklin, Ohio, on September 18, 1886. After graduating from West Point in 1909, he was commissioned a 2nd Lieutenant in the U.S. Army. During World War I, he advanced to the rank of Lieutenant Colonel. In February 1942 he was promoted to the rank of Major General and placed in command of the famous 32nd (Red Arrow) Infantry Division. The general's clothes, uniforms, medals, and military artifacts are on display, as are historical items pertaining to the Franklin area of Ohio.

FORT MEIGS

P.O. Box 3, Perrysburg, OH 43551
Telephone: (419) 874-4037
Curator: Michael Morrell
Hours: Hours vary; longer during summer
Cost of admission: Adults $1.50; children (6 to 12 years) 75¢
Description: Carefully reconstructed Fort Meigs provides the visitor with an opportunity to experience the drama of Ohio's role in the War of 1812. The gatehouse information center offers a brochure detailing a route encompassing the 7 blockhouses, the cannon batteries, and the earthen traverses behind which Harrison's men withstood shot and shell to repulse the British attack. Often called the second War for Independence, the War of 1812 was a brief war. At Fort Meigs a gallant detachment of American troops withstood the siege of British and Canadian troops and Tecumseh's warriors and shattered the enemy threat to the western frontier.

The log walls and blockhouses of Fort Meigs have been reconstructed on the original site.

J. M. DAVIS GUN MUSEUM

P.O. Box 966, 333 N. Lynn Riggs Blvd., Claremore, OK 74017
Telephone: (918) 341-5707
Curator: Lee T. Good
Hours: Monday through Saturday, 8:30 A.M. to 5 P.M.; Sunday 1 P.M. to 5 P.M.; closed Thanksgiving and Christmas

Cost of admission: Free to the public

Description: The J. M. Davis Gun Museum, on Hwy. 66, houses a collection of 20,000 guns; 70 saddles; hundreds of animal horns, trophy heads, and musical instruments; 1,200 steins; and hundreds of swords and knives. On display are such famous weapons as the .44-caliber Walker pistol made for mounted troops, which weighs 4 lbs., 9 oz., and is the heaviest revolving handgun manufactured by Colt and one of Colt's rarest weapons. Rare antique weapons are also on view, among them a case of matched .61-caliber smoothbore rattail dueling pistols with deeply carved and engraved stocks, the locks of which are fine English flintlocks made by Isaac Riviere of London in 1825. Famous military statuary is also on display. The museum is said to possess an example of every firearm used by the military from the Revolutionary period through World War II, with a collection that is still growing.

The J. M. Davis Gun Museum, home of over 20,000 guns and almost as many edged weapons.

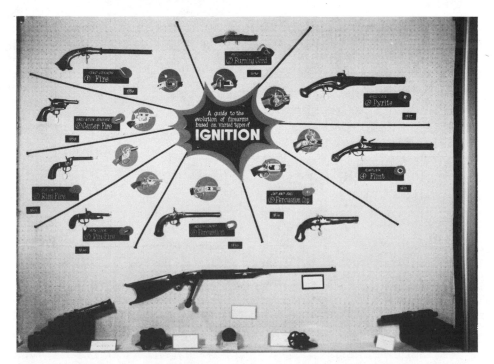

A favorite display shows various types of ignition systems. These begin with the hand cannon, which was invented about 1300, and proceed through major improvements such as the matchlock, flintlock, percussion, breech-loading, pinfire, rimfire, and the centerfire cartridge, used from 1858 to the present time.

FORT CHICKAMAUGA

Cookson, OK 74427
Telephone: (918) 457-5961 or 457-5881
Director: Lt. Col. John H. Jeffries, S.V.R.
Hours: Daily 10 A.M. to 6 P.M.; closed Christmas
Cost of admission: Adults $1.50; children 75¢

Description: This museum provides the visitor with a look at a piece of living history. All displays, saddles, weapons, and other equipment are used in the fort. Fort Chickamauga, under Congressional approval, is the only horse cavalry post still active within the borders of the United States. It is the headquarters for both the 4th United States Cavalry, S.V.R., and headquarters for the 5th Military District, S.V.R. (S.V.R. stands for "Sons of Veterans Reserve," which got its start during the Civil War.) To the full-time troopers garrisoned at the fort, it is a way of life based on hard work, hard training, and busy days practicing the military and social etiquette of the 1870s. The cavalry troopers are first-rate professional soldiers who must meet the exacting standards of the modern rifle manual as well as the 1870 manual. The troopers must qualify as *Expert* in army equitation and use of the lance and the 1861 cavalry saber.

Living history is continually being re-created at Fort Chickamauga. Here a properly uniformed Civil War soldier fires a black powder single-cartridge weapon.

Acting under Congressional approval, Fort Chickamauga is the only horse cavalry post still active within the borders of the United States.

U.S. ARMY FIELD ARTILLERY AND FORT SILL MUSEUM

Fort Sill, OK 73503

Telephone: (405) 351-5123

Curator: Dr. Ronald L. Stewart

Hours: Daily 9 A.M. to 4:30 P.M.; closed December 25–26 and January 1–2

Cost of admission: Free to the public

Description: Fort Sill is 100 miles southwest of Oklahoma City. This museum is said to be one of the most complete and outstanding military museums in the United States. It occupies several of the original buildings of the Old Post, in which are preserved and displayed a host of items depicting the stirring history of the U.S. Field Artillery and the epic Cavalry-Infantry-Indian history of Old Fort Sill. The fort was founded by Gen. Philip H. Sheridan on January 8, 1869, during a winter campaign against the South Plains Indian tribes. The post was constructed by the black troopers of the 10th U.S. Cavalry, the famed "Buffalo Soldiers." Since 1911 Fort Sill has been the home of the U.S. Army Field Artillery Center and School. On the broad firing range of its 94,000-acre military reservation, generations of field artillerymen have learned the art of tube, missile, and aerial gunnery as defenders of the free world.

The Field Artillery Museum building is surrounded by a large and interesting gun park.

"Hunting Horse," the 102-year-old Comanche Indian, a former U.S. Army scout, shows he still knows how to use the bow and arrow; November 8, 1947, at Fort Sill.

Many historic photos are inside the museum. Here the 6th Field Artillery pose with their French-75, which fired the first American shot of World War I.

154

45TH INFANTRY DIVISION MUSEUM

2145 N.E. 36th St., Oklahoma City, OK 73111
Telephone: (405) 424-5313
Director: R. W. Jones
Hours: Tuesday through Friday 9 A.M. to 5 P.M.;
weekends 1 P.M. to 5 P.M.; closed holidays except
Memorial Day, Independence Day, Labor Day, and
Veteran's Day
Cost of admission: Free to the public
Description: The museum is devoted to the history of the citizen soldier from 1830 to the present, with emphasis on the Oklahoma National Guard in general and the 45th Infantry Division in particular. Museum contains items from Hitler's Munich apartment and 213 original cartoons by Bill Mauldin (creator of Willie and Joe) including the famous one: "I can't git no lower Willie, me buttons is in the way!" Also housed are a wide collection of uniforms, weapons, and accouterments of "militia" soldiers and airmen professionally displayed. A 5,000-volume library (for use on premises) includes an archives with unpublished unit historical files

The 45th Division Museum has a memorial to "Willie and Joe," the famed foot soldiers of Bill Mauldin's imagination.

(1952–68), G-2 and G-3 reports of World War II; 10,000 photographs taken by soldiers and professional photographers; 13 World War II and Korean War vehicles (DUKW, half-tracks, etc.); plus a Piper L4b "Grasshopper," all in functioning condition.

FORT CLATSOP NATIONAL MEMORIAL

Rt. 3, Box 604-FC, Astoria, OR 97103
Telephone: (503) 861-2471
Superintendent: Bob Scott
Hours: Daily 8 A.M. to 5 P.M.; summer 8 A.M. to 8 P.M.
Cost of admission: Free to the public
Description: In 1805–6 Meriweather Lewis and William Clark wintered at Fort Clatsop after their journey from the Mississippi River to the Pacific Ocean. Their expedition across the North American continent between the Spanish possessions on the south and British Canada to the north provided the first detailed knowledge of the American northwest. Fort Clatsop was a log stockade 50 feet square located in a thick growth of pine. Two rows of cabins (3 rooms on the west side and 4 on the east) were separated by a parade ground. A visitor center/museum reveals artifacts and relates the story with audiovisuals and showcases.

Fort Clatsop, a log stockade 50 feet square, is located in a thick growth of pine.

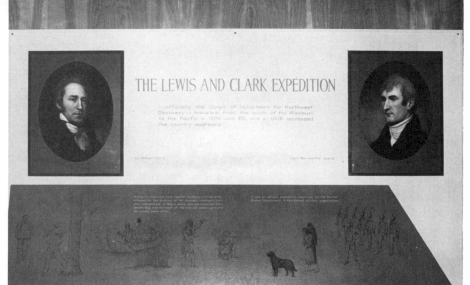

Inside the small fort are exhibits, artifacts, and memorabilia of the Lewis and Clark Expedition.

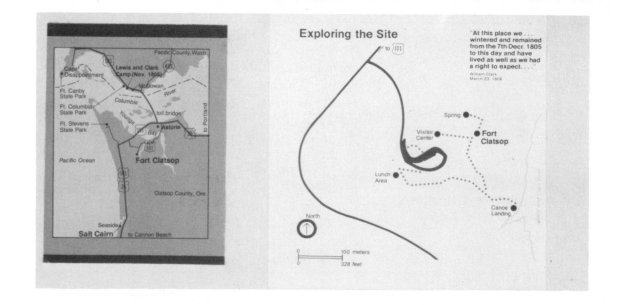

FORT DALLES SURGEON'S QUARTERS

15th and Garrison, The Dalles, OR 97058
Telephone: (503) 296-4547
Director: Wasco County, City of The Dalles Museum Commission
Hours: May through October, Tuesday through Friday 10:30 A.M. to 5 P.M.; Saturday and Sunday 10 A.M. to 5 P.M. October through May, Wednesday through Friday noon to 4 P.M.; Saturday and Sunday 10 A.M. to 4 P.M.; closed legal holidays
Cost of admission: Free to the public

Description: Fort Dalles, first established as Camp Drum in 1850, was the only post between Fort Vancouver and Fort Laramie. It became Fort Drum in 1853, then was named Fort Dalles in 1855. The fort was abandoned in 1867. Fort Dalles Surgeon's Quarters is the only remaining building. The original Surgeon's Quarters have been turned into a museum containing numerous interesting military artifacts and pieces of equipment.

Exhibit of guns in the upstairs north room.

Fort Dalles Surgeon's Quarters.

157

FORT STEVENS MUSEUM AND INTERPRETIVE CENTER

Fort Stevens State Park, Historical Area, Hammond, OR 97121

Telephone: (503) 861-2000

Curator: Susan M. Scully

Hours: Weekdays, October to May 8 A.M. to 4 P.M.; June to September 10 A.M. to 6 P.M.; holidays 10 A.M. to 6 P.M.

Cost of admission: Free to the public

Description: Fort Stevens Museum and Interpretive Center provides the tourist with description and diagrams of the construction and activities of Fort Stevens as a military installation, 1865–1947. On display are projectiles of various sizes, uniforms, personal articles of the soldiers, and photo albums of the men stationed here. There are also brief movies of the 10-inch DC rifles and 12-inch mortars during target practice. The Historical Area also has on display two 5-inch .38-caliber rifles and two 3-inch .50-caliber rifles, so the visitor can visualize the batteries when they were active. Due to open shortly is the 1911 guardhouse, which will serve as a living history museum, concentrating on the personal life of a soldier.

Battlements at Fort Stevens, which was built at the mouth of the Columbia River in 1862 to protect the river from Confederate gun boats. One of Oregon's most popular parks, it has picnic facilities and is equipped with hundreds of sites for overnight camping.

Fort Stevens State Park, on the northern Oregon coast in Clatsop County, today includes the historic remains of old Fort Stevens, a military installation established during the Civil War by the U.S. Army. Battery Russell, shown here, was the last concrete gun emplacement constructed. It was completed in 1904 and was deactivated in 1944. It was the last installation of its type within the continental U.S. to be active, and the only one which was fired upon by the enemy during World War II. This scene shows 1 of 2 large 10-foot rifles at Battery Russell being fired during a practice exercise in the 1930s. All guns have been removed, but Battery Russell has been partially restored by the state and is open to visitors.

The Guardhouse (1908). Recently restored, it serves as an annex to the museum and as a living history tribute to the men who were stationed at Fort Stevens.

PENNSYLVANIA MILITARY MUSEUM

28th Division Shrine, Box 148, Boalsburg, PA
16827
Telephone: (814) 466-6263
Curator: Donald J. Morrison
Hours: Summer, Wednesday through Saturday 9
A.M. to 5 P.M.; winter, Wednesday through Saturday
10 A.M. to 4:30 P.M.; Sunday, noon to 4:30 P.M.
Cost of admission: Adults (12 and over) $1; senior
citizens; educational groups free

A World War I battle scene, complete with sound effects, Pennsylvania Military Museum.

A World War I National Guard exhibit.

Description: The museum's midstate location and accessibility to main roads make it easy to visit. It and the 28th Division Shrine are located on U.S. 322 in Boalsburg, just east of State College. The first military units in Pennsylvania were established in 1747, when Benjamin Franklin organized the Battalion of Associations in anticipation of the need to defend the province as conditions on the frontier became more unsettled. The insignias of the many troops that formed the Associations are shown in the initial exhibit. Other exhibits explain events of the French and Indian War of the 1750s. The War for Independence is highlighted by a diorama. Another of the numerous dioramas portrays the War of 1812. The Mexican War is represented, as is the Civil War, the Spanish-American War, the two World Wars, Korea, and Vietnam.

U.S. ARMY MILITARY HISTORY INSTITUTE

Carlisle Barracks, PA 17013
Telephone: (717) 245-3152
Director: Col. Donald P. Shaw
Hours: Daily 8 A.M. to 4:30 P.M.
Cost of admission: Free to the public
Description: This is the Army's official repository for military history. The institute contains a library, manuscript archives, photo archives, research and reference staff, and *two museums:* the Omar N. Bradley Museum and the Hessian Powder Magazine Museum. In 1968 Gen. Omar Bradley offered his personal papers and memorabilia to the Army. In accepting General Bradley's offer, the Secretary of the Army directed that the papers become a part of the U.S. military history research exhibit developed to portray General Bradley's career in the Army. In 1948 the Hessian Powder Magazine was officially opened to the public as the post museum. While viewing the museum visitors will see displays in the order that events occurred in the Revolutionary War, the Civil War, and school era at Carlisle Barracks.

Upton Hall, U.S. Army Military History Institute and Omar Bradley Museum, Carlisle Barracks, Pa.

Interior, Omar Bradley museum.

The Hessian Powder Magazine Museum.

Interior, Hessian Powder Magazine Museum.

BRANDYWINE BATTLEFIELD STATE PARK

P.O. Box 202, Chadds Ford, PA 19317
Telephone: (215) 459-3342
Acting Curator: Frank J. Schmidt
Hours: Daily 9 A.M. to dusk
Cost of admission: Free to the public
Description: Off U.S. 1, near Kennett Square, Pa., the Brandywine Battlefield Site has a visitor center that possesses exhibits relating the story of the battle and its role in the Revolution. In late August of 1777, during the third year of the War for Independence, Gen. William Howe with 15,000 British and Hessian troops landed at the head of the Elk in Maryland. His plan was to march from there to Philadelphia and occupy that city. Standing between the combined British and Hessian army and their goal was Washington with 14,000 men on the east side of Brandywine Creek. Included in the exhibit is a display of weapons and military accouterments either used in the battle or of the type used during that period. There are also excavated objects, plus two historic houses used as quarters for Generals Washington and Lafayette before the battle; these are furnished with period artifacts.

Headquarters for Washington, prior to the battle of Brandywine, were in this low-ceilinged, sparsely furnished room.

FORT NECESSITY NATIONAL BATTLEFIELD

The National Pike, Farmington, PA 15437
Telephone: (412) 329-5512
Superintendent: Robert L. Warren
Hours: Daily 8:30 A.M. to 5 P.M. (extended in summer); closed Christmas and New Year's Day
Cost of admission: Free to the public
Description: The visitor center/museum shows the history of Fort Necessity. Lt. Col. George Washington, in command of about 160 Virginia volunteers, arrived at Great Meadows on May 24, 1754. For nearly 2 months this untrained, poorly provisioned army had been hauling supplies and heavy equipment all the way from Alexandria, Va., much of the way over narrow mountain trails. Here at Great Meadows there were winding streams that provided natural entrenchments, and after bushes along the stream banks had been cut, Washington wrote Governor Dinwiddie that he had here "a charming field for an encounter." This area then became the site of the future Fort Necessity.

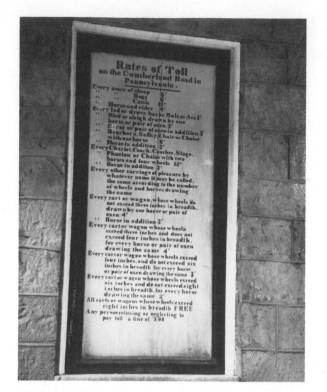

Sign on Toll House on old U.S. 40 east of Fort Necessity at Addison, Pa.

The opening battle of the war fought by England and France for control of North America occurred at Fort Necessity, on July 3, 1754. The action at Fort Necessity was also the first major event in the military career of George Washington, and it marked the only time he would be forced to surrender to an enemy.

GETTYSBURG NATIONAL MILITARY PARK

Gettysburg, PA 17325
Telephone: (717) 334-1124
Director: Larry Eckert
Hours: Daily 8 A.M. to 5 P.M.; closed Thanksgiving,
Christmas, and New Year's Day
Cost of admission: Free to the public

Description: Civil War Union and Confederate military equipment including shoulder arms, sidearms, edged weapons, cartridges, artillery projectiles, uniforms, insignia, flags, surgical and medical implements, paintings, and photographs are on display. This site marks the greatest battle of the Civil War, taking place July 1–3, 1863. The more numerous Union Army lost 23,000 men: killed, wounded, or missing. Confederate forces lost 20,000, although this number is open to debate. Both commanding generals have been criticized for their tactics: Lee for his reliance on unseasoned commanders and for his authorization of Pickett's charge; Meade for his failure to organize a massive counterattack and his failure to pursue the fleeing enemy.

Aerial view of Gettysburg.

BUSHY RUN BATTLEFIELD

Jeannette, PA 15644
Telephone: (412) 527-5584
Site Administrator: Sean Fitzpatrick
Hours: Winter, Tuesday through Saturday 9 A.M. to 4:30 P.M., Sunday noon to 4:30 P.M.; summer 9 A.M. to 8 P.M., Sunday noon to 8 P.M.; closed most federal and state holidays
Cost of admission: Adults (12 to 60 years) 50¢
Description: Bushy Run Battlefield's 190 acres enclose the site of Col. Henry Bouquet's victory over Indian forces of Pontiac's War. The battle was fought August 5–6, 1763. The terrain, which influenced the tactics of the combatants, is much as it was in 1763. Understanding of the battle is aided by the design of the reforested areas and will be further improved by a self-guided tour, under development. The visitor center contains artifacts, maps, and graphics panels to orient the visitor to the period and the battlefield. Tours for school and other groups are available by appointment.

FORT LIGONIER

S. Market St., Ligonier, PA 15658
Telephone: (412) 238-9701
Executive Director: L. W. Stear
Hours: Daily 9 A.M. to 5 P.M.; summer 9 A.M. to 7 P.M.
Cost of admission: Adults $3, children $1.50
Description: Fort Ligonier was named for Sir John (Jean Louis) Ligonier, field marshal and commander-in-chief of the British Army. A French Huguenot, Ligonier went to England as a young man, volunteered in the army, and rose through the ranks to become Britain's highest ranking military officer. In 1766 Fort Ligonier was decommissioned and a civil commandant, Arthur St. Clair, was placed in charge. The fort was used in 1744 as a refuge for local settlers during the Indian raids of Lord Dunmore's War. One wing of the museum houses a permanent exhibit of artifacts from the many battles fought at this site, as well as dioramas depicting phases of the action. A large new wing houses changing exhibits of weaponry and other items relating to the military.

Inside the palisade at Fort Ligonier.

Within the museum life-size mannequins tell a story.

THE DANDY FIRST MUSEUM

*103rd Engineer Battalion, 3205 Lancaster Ave.,
Philadelphia, PA 19104*
Telephone: (215) 222-8117 or 222-8118
Curator: Capt. J. Craig Nannos
Hours: By appointment only
Cost of admission: Free to the public

Description: The museum features artifacts, paintings, accouterments, weapons, and uniforms showing the history of this battalion from 1777 to the present. Artifacts include the Revolutionary War, Civil War, Spanish-American War, World War I, and World War II. The collection has some fine mid– to late–19th-century paintings plus a fine display of uniforms from the Civil War up to and including the present time.

WAR LIBRARY AND MUSEUM

Military Order of the Loyal Legion of the United States, 1805 Pine St., Philadelphia, PA 19103
Telephone: (215) 735-8196
Curator: Russ A. Pritchard
Hours: Monday through Friday 10 A.M. to 4 P.M.
Cost of admission: $1

Description: The reputation of the War Library and Museum is based on its extensive artifact collection and 12,000 books relating to the events preceding the Civil War, the conflict itself, and the early reconstruction. Highlights of the collection include two life masks of Lincoln by Volk and Mills; a dress uniform and presentation sword of Gen. U.S. Grant; a field uniform, presentation sword, and revolver of Gen. George G. Meade; and a presentation sword of Gen. Francis P. Blair. In addition, there are a number of period flags and guidons; a selection of handguns, long arms, and edged weapons; uniforms and relics covering most aspects of the Civil War; plus numerous personal items.

FORT PITT MUSEUM

Point State Park, Pittsburgh, PA 15222
Telephone: (412) 281-9284
Director: Robert J. Trombetta
Hours: Wednesday through Saturday 10 A.M. to 4:30 P.M.; Sunday noon to 4:30 P.M.; closed legal holidays
Cost of admission: Adults $1.50

Description: Exhibits re-create life on the frontier during the second half of the 18th century. Of special interest is the 15-foot-diameter model of Fort Pitt and a life-size, fully stocked trader's

Front of Fort Pitt Museum.

cabin. The museum offers 70 permanent exhibits and a series of changing exhibits, plus a 20-minute orientation film. The Royal American Regiment performs in the park on Sunday afternoons during the summer.

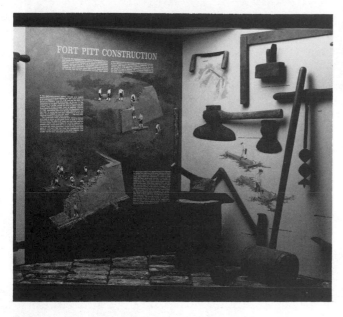

A tribute to the English officer on the frontier.

A display showing how Fort Pitt was constructed.

THE EAGLE GUN MUSEUM

R.D. 2, Strasburg, PA 17579

Telephone: (717) 687-7931

Curator and Owner: Vincent W. Nolt

Hours: Daily, with hours varying according to time of year

Cost of admission: Adults $1.75; children (6 to 11 years) 50¢

Description: The Eagle Gun Museum is located on Rt. 741, west of Strasburg, Pa. The original building was built around 1740 by John Herr, a relative of the man who was Lancaster County's first settler. The land grant is recorded in the year of 1710. The museum houses one of the finest collections of Pennsylvania-Kentucky rifles and other weapons, from the crossbow through World War II. Few people realize that the superbly accurate, beautifully made, misnamed Kentucky rifle of early American history was developed in south-central Pennsylvania. Here in the Lancaster County area, the gunmaker's art and superb craftsmanship reached its peak between 1725 and 1875, which saw the close of the flintlock and percussion period of firearms. More than 300 gunsmiths are known to have made rifles in Lancaster County during this time.

Exterior of the Eagle Gun Museum.

VALLEY FORGE NATIONAL HISTORICAL PARK

Valley Forge, PA 19481
Telephone: (215) 783-7700, Ext. 71
Curator: E. M. Browning
Hours: Daily 8:30 A.M. to 5 P.M.; summer 8:30 A.M. to 6 P.M.
Cost of admission: Free to the public
Description: Just outside the suburbs of Philadelphia, the park has a museum showing approximately 1,500 Revolutionary War items. Included are muskets, rifles, swords, pole arms, handbooks, diaries, eating utensils, medical equipment, and other accessories; furnished historic houses are open to the public. (Washington's headquarters building is open daily; General Varnum's headquarters is open when staffing is available.) Fortifications and replicas of the soldiers' huts are visible on the outer line drive. General Washington's sleeping marquee is on display in the visitor center as well.

Light artillery cannon positioned as they were during the Revolutionary War.

The reality of cold and snow may be seen by those who visit Valley Forge in the winter.

General Washington's sleeping marquee.

FORT LE BOEUF MUSEUM

123 S. High St., Waterford, PA 16441
Telephone: (814) 796-4113
Curator: Ms. Patricia A. Leiphart
Hours: Hours vary according to season
Cost of admission: Adults (12 to 65 years) $1

Description: The museum of Fort LeBoeuf in Waterford dramatically reflects the struggle between France and Britain for colonial empire, as well as the later triumph of an independent America. The site's strategic location on the waters of the upper Ohio made it of vital importance in the struggle for control of the wilderness in the early 18th century. As the French were later displaced by the British, and the British in turn by Americans, the position along French Creek became the site of 3 successive forts. This museum interprets the French and Indian War period using displays and multimedia presentations. No fort remains are visible, but the museum is adjacent to the original fort site.

The museum displays over 1,500 Revolutionary War items.

ARTILLERY COMPANY OF NEWPORT MUSEUM

23 Clark St., Newport, RI 02840
Telephone: (401) 846-8488
Curator: Lt. Col. Elton Manuel
Hours: Daily 11 A.M. to 4 P.M.
Cost of admission: Donations only
Description: The Artillery Company Museum is said to possess one of the most outstanding collections of foreign and domestic militaria to be seen in the United States. Started 20 years ago, it has grown from a minute collection to represent 104 countries throughout the world. Within the walls of the old armory, built in 1836, some 90 years after the company was chartered, are displayed a number of historic items. A letter addressed to the company dated 1794 and signed by George Washington is a prized possession. A colored lithograph of the "Battle Of Lake Erie" is framed with wood from Commodore Oliver Hazard Perry's flagship *Lawrence*.

Members of the Newport Artillery Museum pose with 1 of the 4 Revolutionary War cannons in their possession.

COWPENS NATIONAL BATTLEFIELD

Chesnee, SC

Address inquiries to: Kings Mountain National Military Park, P.O. Box 31, Kings Mountain, NC 28086

Cost of admission: Free to the public

Description: Cowpens National Battlefield is located 11 miles northwest of I-85 and Gaffney, S.C., and 2 miles southeast of U.S. 221 and Chesnee, S.C. The battlefield is at the intersection of S.C. 11 and S.C. 110. A major expansion and development of the battlefield is now underway. On January 17, 1781, American militia commanded by Daniel Morgan inflicted heavy losses on a British force under Sir Banastre Tarleton—a serious blow to Cornwallis's plans for the conquest of the Carolinas. A visitor center (museum), walking trails, a motor tour road, and wayside exhibits are to be seen. Many valuable paintings and military artifacts are on view at the visitors' center.

Painting of the Battle of Cowpens.

General Daniel Morgan, the American commander at Cowpens, by C. W. Peale.

FORT SUMTER AND FORT MOULTRIE

Drawer R, Sullivan's Island, SC 29482
Telephone: (803) 883-3123
Superintendent: W. P. Crawford
Hours: Daily 8 A.M. to 5 P.M.; summer 8 A.M. to 6 P.M.; closed Christmas
Cost of admission: Free to the public
Description: There are 2 areas that make up this one National Park Service site. The first, Fort Sumter, is reached by tour boat; the second, Fort Moultrie, can be reached by automobile. The forts lie opposite one another as twin

Two 15-inch Rodman cannons (in foreground), Fort Sumter.

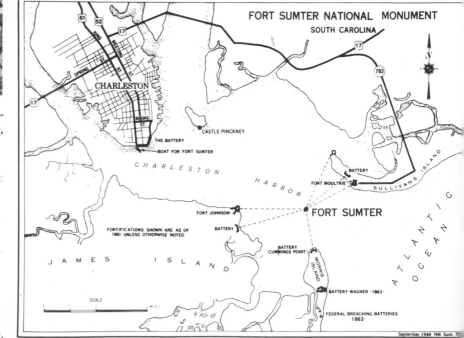

Fort Moultrie Visitor Center.

"The housetops in Charleston during the bombardment of Fort Sumter," from *Harper's Weekly,* May 4, 1861.

Area map of Fort Sumter.

170

guardians to the harbor at Charleston, S.C. While many historic areas concentrate on a particular period in time, the story of Fort Moultrie and Fort Sumter is one which spans 171 years. From the Revolution through World War II, coastal fortifications were this nation's first line of national defense. There actually have been 3 Fort Moultries. The first was constructed in 1776, and was still incomplete when it defeated a fleet of 9 English warships on June 28, 1776. Fort Sumter was begun in 1829, and it was at this site, on April 12, 1861, the first shot of the Civil War was fired. Each of the forts houses a collection of military artifacts that illustrate a great span in this nation's military history.

OLD FORT MEADE MUSEUM

Address inquiries to: P.O. Box 134, Fort Meade, SD 57741

Telephone: (605) 347-9822

Vice President: Ralph P. Hackert

Hours: Daily 9 A.M. to 5 P.M.; Sunday 1 P.M. to 6 P.M.

Cost of admission: Donations only

Description: Many items on display show the mission of Fort Meade as "The Peacekeeper Fort," among them a diorama of Bear Butte (several miles north of Fort Meade), as seen when Custer's expedition toured the Black Hills in 1874, 2 years before he was killed in June of 1876 at the Battle of the Little Big Horn in Montana. One room of exhibits relates to the first residents in this area, the Indians; other displays show the participation of the 7th Cavalry at Custer's last stand; the 7th Cavalry coming to start Fort Meade from Fort Abraham Lincoln near Mandan, N.D., in 1878 (they left in 1888); the Reno court-martial story; the adoption of "The Star Spangled Banner" here (documented from National Archives), and the story of the 4th Cavalry and other units that were here until Fort Meade became a veterans hospital.

FORT SISSETON STATE PARK, MUSEUM, AND VISITOR CENTER

Lake City, SD 57247

Telephone: (605) 448-5474

Park Manager: Rick Collignon; Program Coordinator: Jessica Giusti

Hours: Daily 10 A.M. to 8 P.M.

Cost of admission: May through September $2

Description: The Minnesota Indian uprising in 1862 demonstrated the need for a fort to provide military protection to the settlers in this region. Fort Sisseton was established in 1864. In addition to the museum, there is an annual historical festival. Muzzleloaders rendezvous at the post and compete in such events as a clay-pigeon shoot and a tomahawk-throwing contest. Drill parades, wagon rides, fiddling contests, square dancing, and frontier craftsmanship are some of the features of this popular festival.

Fort Sisseton.

FORT DONELSON NATIONAL MILITARY PARK

P.O. Box F, Dover, TN 37058
Telephone: (615) 232-5348
Director: E. J. Pratt
Hours: Daily 8 A.M. to 4 P.M.; closed Christmas Day
Cost of admission: Free to the public
Description: Fort Donelson is 1 mile west of Dover, and 3 miles east of Land Between the Lakes on U.S. 79. The visitor center/museum is open daily. Soldiers and slaves built this 15-acre fort over a period of 7 months. They used axes and shovels to make a wall of logs and earth 10 feet high. The fort's purpose was to protect the Cumberland River batteries from land attack. The reconstructed huts are representative of the 400-plus that stood on or near this site at the time of the battle. There are exhibits and audiovisual displays explaining the Battle of Fort

One of the many outdoor memorials to Civil War heroes at Fort Donelson National Military Park.

Donelson, February 1862, which resulted in a major Union victory. The visitor center/museum also houses many Civil War artifacts.

CARTER HOUSE MILITARY MUSEUM

1140 Columbia Ave., Franklin, TN 37064
Telephone: (615) 794-1733
Curator: Dolores Kestner
Hours: Monday through Saturday 9 A.M. to 4 P.M.;
Sunday 2 P.M. to 4 P.M.; closed holidays
Cost of admission: Adults $1.50; children under 16 years 50¢
Description: The Carter House is one of the state's most compelling historic landmarks, in its simplicity and unique position in history—a house caught in the swirling center of one of the bloodiest battles of the War Between the States. The military museum, which is housed in the basement, holds treasures of the past, including interesting documents, uniforms, flags, guns, and maps of the battlefield; as well as pictures of heroes and reproductions of the famous Civil War prints by Gilbert Gaul, and many other items of historic value.

Entrance to the Carter House Military Museum.

STONES RIVER NATIONAL BATTLEFIELD

Rt. 10, Box 401, Old Nashville Hwy.,
Murfreesboro, TN 37130
Telephone: (615) 893-9501
Superintendent: James A. Sanders
Hours: Daily 8 A.M. to 5 P.M.; closed Christmas
Cost of admission: Free to the public
Description: Stones River National Battlefield is in the northwest corner of Murfreesboro, Tenn., 27 miles southeast of Nashville. At dawn on December 31, 1862, the Confederates charged the Union right flank. There was the roar of musketry and the deep boom of cannon as the onslaught sent the Federals reeling backwards through the dense cedar thickets which covered the battlefield. The noise was so intense that Confederate soldiers paused in their attack to stuff their ears with cotton. At the Nashville Pike the Union forces held. At that point they beat off attack after attack with cannon and rifle, and with bayonet and clubbed musket when the ammunition ran out. By late afternoon reserves arrived and a new line was established along the pike. The day's fighting sputtered to a close.

An old soldier salutes an old soldier hero.

Light artillery.

An artillery caisson.

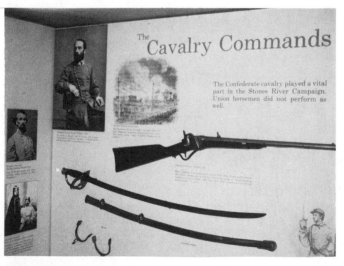

The story of cavalry.

The story of artillery.

TENNESSEE STATE MUSEUM, MILITARY HISTORY BRANCH

War Memorial Bldg., Nashville, TN 37219
Telephone: (615) 741-2692
Director: Dr. Ellsworth Brown

Hours: Tuesday through Saturday 9 A.M. to 5 P.M.; Sunday and Monday 1 P.M. to 5 P.M.; closed Thanksgiving, Christmas, New Year's Day and Easter
Cost of admission: Free to the public
Description: The museum features exhibits on the Spanish-American War, World War I, and

Tennessee State Museum poster.

World War II. Spanish-American War artifacts include a deck gun from the *Nashville* (which fired the first shot), weapons and uniforms, a soldier's belongings, Moro and Bagobo tribal weapons and crafts, and souvenirs of the USS *Maine;* World War I items include the uniform and medals of Sgt. Alvin C. York, gas warfare equipment, weapons and uniforms, war souvenirs and memorabilia; World War II displays include the medals and uniforms of Tennessee heroes and heroines, an exhibit on the atomic bomb, German and Japanese as well as Allied uniforms and weapons, war posters, and propaganda materials. The Main Tennessee State Museum, housed in the James K. Polk Cultural Center, has exhibits on the Revolutionary War, War of 1812, Mexican War, and Civil War.

"Tennesseans at War" exhibit displays uniforms worn by both men and women.

Preparing a special case entitled "Wolves of the Sea."

175

SHILOH NATIONAL MILITARY PARK

Shiloh, TN 38376
Telephone: (901) 689-5275
Superintendent: Zeb V. McKinney
Hours: Daily 8 A.M. to 5 P.M.; closed Christmas
Cost of admission: Free to the public

Description: The bitter battle fought here April 6–7, 1862, prepared the way for Maj. Gen. U.S. Grant's successful siege of Vicksburg. The battle left many mementos, a great collection of which are housed inside the visitor center and throughout the park. The collection includes rare handguns, such as a Colt Navy .36 Model 1851, and a Starr Army .44 of about 1860, plus other weapons such as cavalry sabers, rifles, carbines, and bayonets. Uniforms, boots, caps, flags, battle streamers, haversacks, cartridge boxes, belt buckles, and sword-belt plates are all to be seen. Maps, audiovisuals, and motion pictures explain the bloody battle.

Confederate guns at Shiloh point toward the Sunken Road.

Young Confederate enlisted men from the Washington Artillery of New Orleans, prior to the Battle of Shiloh.

TEXAS NATIONAL GUARD HISTORY CENTER

Camp Mabry, Austin, TX 78756
Telephone: (512) 475-5059
Curator: SSG Joe L. Todd
Hours: Varying hours
Cost of admission: Free to the public

Description: The center features displays from the Texas militia days of the Texas Revolution. Some artifacts and memorabilia consist of fire-arms from 1528, when a Spanish ship was wrecked on the coast; and relics of warring Comanche, Apache, and other Indian tribes that did not welcome the coming of settlers. Missions, rather than forts, were established and it was around these that militiamen first rallied. The Spanish, French, and English all attempted to conquer Texas, and their marks are shown in this museum. Uniforms, small arms, handguns, and other items of combat are on display. The Civil War is well represented, as are World War I and World War II.

FORT DAVIS NATIONAL HISTORIC SITE

P.O. Box 1456, Fort Davis, TX 79734
Telephone: (915) 426-3225
Hours: Daily, winter 8 A.M. to 5 P.M.; summer 8 A.M. to 6 P.M.
Cost of admission: $1.50 per car or 50¢ per person
Description: The museum is located on the northern edge of the town of Fort Davis, Tex. It can be reached from U.S. 290 on the north and U.S. 90 on the south from Tex. 17 and Tex. 118. The museum tells the history of the fort from 1854 to 1891, displaying military, Indian, and civilian artifacts of the period. Major exhibits are a diorama depicting Grierson's Raid at Quitman Canyon and an M1875 Gatling gun with limber; there are numerous other displays. The fort was the key post in the defense system of west Texas. Fort Davis played a major role in the history of the southwestern frontier. From 1854 to 1891, troops based at the post guarded immigrants, freighters, and stagecoaches on the San Antonio-El Paso road and fought off hostile Indians.

Officers' quarters of the key post in the west Texas defensive system.

Negro troops of the 24th and 25th Infantry, as well as the 9th and 10th Cavalry, were at Fort Davis.

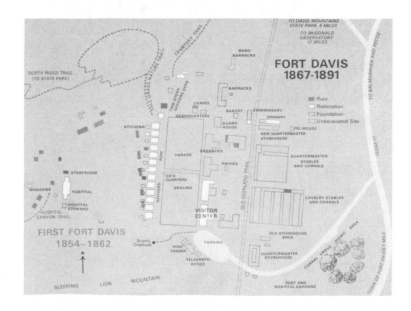

177

PATE MUSEUM OF TRANSPORTATION

P.O. Box 711, Fort Worth, TX 76101
Telephone: (817) 332-1161
Curator: Jim Peel
*Hours: Tuesday through Sunday 9 A.M. to 5 P.M.;
closed holidays*
Cost of admission: Free to the public
Description: The Pate Museum displays the Minesweeper Boat #5, adjacent to which is the museum's Navy F9F jet with wings in position for storage on an aircraft carrier. Other aircraft exhibits range from helicopters to transports to fighter planes. The Pate Museum also features changing space exhibits from NASA and the Smithsonian Institution. Ship models, classic automobiles (such as an Oldsmobile Replica 1901, an Oakland Touring 1910, and an Austin London Taxi 1955), an Army Air Force "Gooney Bird," and a C-119 Flying Boxcar are among the displays.

Front entrance to Pate Museum.

178

GALVESTON COUNTY HISTORICAL MUSEUM

P.O. Box 1047, 2219 Market St., Galveston, TX 77553

Telephone: (713) 766-2340

Director: Kirk D. Lyons

Hours: Monday through Friday 8:30 A.M. to 4 P.M.; Saturday 9 A.M. to 4:30 P.M.; Sunday 1 P.M. to 5 P.M.; closed holidays

Cost of admission: Free to the public

Description: The Galveston County Historical Museum was founded to preserve and exhibit the history of this coastal area. Exhibits feature Galveston in the Civil War, Austin's colonists, and the men and ship of the Texas navy. Other displays focus on the cities, towns, and events of Galveston County, including the Texas disaster of 1947. The rise and fall of the "Wall Street of the Southwest" and the heyday of gambling are also shown here.

CONFEDERATE RESEARCH CENTER AND GUN MUSEUM

P.O. Box 619, Hill Jr. College, Hillsboro, TX 76645

Telephone: (817) 582-2555

Curator: Dr. H. B. Simpson

Hours: Daily 8 A.M. to 5 P.M.

Cost of admission: Free to the public

Description: Sponsored by the Texas State Gun Collectors' Association, the center houses two rotating collections of firearms and edged weapons and a permanent collection of handguns, shoulder arms, edged weapons, ammunition, and artifacts. A library of 3,500 books, including official records of the Army and Navy, are also housed here, as are 1,500 bound volumes including the Southern Historical Society papers. The microfilm library includes service records of all 6,000 members of Hood's Texas Brigade, many Texas newspapers published during the 1850s and 1860s, post returns of the U.S. forts in Texas, and the 1860 census reports of central Texas counties. Numerous dioramas, figurines, paintings, etchings, lithographs, and woodcarvings are also part of the museum.

Library and entrance to gun museum at Confederate Research Center.

FORT BELKNAP MUSEUM AND ARCHIVES

P.O. Box 68, Newcastle, TX 76372
Telephone: (817) 549-1856
Curator: Asst. Archivist Barbara Ledbetter
Hours: Thursday through Tuesday 9 A.M. to 5 P.M.;
closed Thanksgiving, Christmas, and New Year's
Day
Cost of admission: Free to the public
Description: The museum is located 3 miles south of Newcastle, Tex., on Hwys. 251, 24, Fm. 61.

This U.S. Army frontier post was established in 1851 by Brig. Gen. William Goldsmith Belknap. It was one of the most important of its time and proved to be the hub of a network of roads from north, south, east, and west, including the famous Butterfield Overland Mail and Stage Line through Fort Belknap. It was abandoned as an army post in 1867. Restoration commenced during the Texas Centennial in 1936. Just inside the arched gateway is seen the native conglomerate rock holding the bronze plaque from the U.S. Department of Interior recognizing Fort Belknap as a National Historic Landmark. In the distance is the fort commissary, which now houses the museum.

Looking inside the main gate of Fort Belknap. On the right is a boulder with a historic bronze plaque. Beyond, to the left, is the museum building.

FORT CONCHO MUSEUM

213 E. Ave. D, San Angelo, TX 76903
Telephone: (916) 655-9121
Director: John F. Vaughan
Hours: Monday through Saturday 9 A.M. to 5 P.M.;
Sunday 1 P.M. to 5 P.M.; closed Christmas Eve,
Christmas, and New Year's Day
Cost of admission: Adults $1; children 50¢
Description: This frontier fort has 14 original buildings and 4 reconstructed buildings. Exhibits feature military history of the Plains Indians and their wars against Union soldiers. Interiors of rooms, offices, barracks, and hospital are complete in many details, with uniforms, weapons, and belongings of the original military contingent. In the latter part of the 19th century a chain of military posts was built across Texas. The fort built near the convergence of the North and Middle Concho rivers was established in 1867 as Camp Hatch and became Fort Concho in 1868. It was an important center for men and supplies used in military campaigns that eventually led to the settlement of the "Indian Wars" in this region. The famous Buffalo Soldiers—the all-black 9th and 10th Cavalry regiments—were garrisoned here for a short time.

Headquarters building at Fort Concho.

Interior of court-martial room, headquarters building.

THE ALAMO

Alamo Plaza, San Antonio, TX 78205
Telphone: (512) 225-3853
Curator: Charles J. Long
Hours: Monday through Saturday 9 A.M. to 5:30
P.M.; Sunday 10 A.M. to 5:30 P.M.; closed
Christmas Eve and Christmas Day
Cost of admission: Free to the public
Description: This shrine, a former mission church, commemorates the various heroes killed in the 1836 battle. The Long Barrack Museum has visual aid machines and displays which give the history of the men, times, and events of Spanish through Republic of Texas periods.

The museum contains many historical objects that for various reasons do not fit into other buildings. The visual aid machines offer a 10-minute movie and three 6-minute self-operating slide shows telling the history of the Alamo under Spain and Mexico, the 1836 battle, and the Alamo's preservation under the Daughters of the Republic of Texas. Heroes such as Jim Bowie, Davy Crockett, William Travis, and Jim Bonham helped make the Alamo famous and gave their lives in the process. In the southwest corner of the gardens is the Texas History Library. It contains valuable historic books, documents, maps, manuscripts, artwork, and memorabilia spanning 4 centuries of Texas history.

The Alamo as it looks today.

TEXAS RANGER HALL OF FAME AND MUSEUM AT FORT FISHER PARK

P.O. Box 1370, Waco, TX 76703
Telephone: (817) 754-1433
Curator: Gaines de Graffenried
Hours: Daily 9 A.M. to 5 P.M.; closed Thanksgiving, Christmas, and New Year's Day
Cost of admission: Adults $2.50; children over 6 years $1.50
Description: Many famous guns are collected here—one of Jim Bowie's rifles, Bonnie and Clyde's guns, Billy the Kid's gun, and many others. Dioramas depicting the history of the Texas Rangers, a library, and an art gallery are open to visitors. The Texas Ranger Hall of Fame and Fort Fisher Museum are two vivid military displays that will be talked about and remembered for a long time. The two house some of the most valuable guns of the old West and other military memorabilia. Both are located at the intersection of I-35 and the Brazos River (Lake Brazos).

Front entrance to Texas Ranger Hall of Fame.

At one time the Texas Rangers were state militia. This museum reveals their history in exciting visual form.

FORT DOUGLAS MUSEUM OF MILITARY HISTORY

U.S. Army Support Detachment, Salt Lake, Fort Douglas, UT 84113

Telephone: (801) 524-4154

Curator: Gen. Kaufmann, USA (Ret.)

Hours: Daily 10 A.M. to 4:30 P.M.; closed holidays

Cost of admission: Free to the public

Description: The Fort Douglas Museum tells the story of the U.S. Army in Utah and the inter-mountain West. Emphasis is on the Civil War era and on the fort from 1876 to 1880. The collection consists of material from the following eras: 18th-century Spanish military explorers; Civil War in the West; the Utah War (1857–58); minorities in the army (19th century); World War I; and the World War II Fort Douglas prisoner of war camp.

Fort Douglas Museum building.

Uniforms such as these are to be seen at the museum. Memorabilia from U.S. wars up to and including World War II are on display.

184

HUBBARDTON BATTLEFIELD SITE

Hubbardton, VT 05749
Telephone: (802) 828-3226
Superintendent: John P. Dumville
Hours: Daily 9:30 A.M. to 5:30 P.M.
Cost of admission: Free to the public
Description: The Hubbardton Battlefield is the site of the only Revolutionary War battle fought in Vermont. Constructed in 1970, a visitor reception/museum center houses a lounge and an audiovisual room. A diorama constructed by Vermont artist Paul V. Winters in 1963 is also on display. This fine creative work shows the Battle of Hubbardton in its furious early stages. Thorough research enabled the artist to depict historically accurate details in uniforms, equipment, troop positions, and terrain. The diorama offers museum visitors a unique perspective of history in three dimensions.

Hubbardton Battle Monument.

VERMONT NATIONAL GUARD MUSEUM

Bldg. 25, Camp Johnson, Winooski, VT 05404
Telephone: (202) 655-0270, Ext. 72
Curator: Roger C. Nyce
Hours: Monday through Friday 9 A.M. to 4 P.M.;
first Saturday of each month 9 A.M. to 4 P.M.;
holidays on request
Cost of admission: Free to the public
Description: The museum contains artifacts and memorabilia of the Vermont Militia-Guard from the periods of the Revolutionary War, the Civil War, the Spanish-American War, and the wars and involvements of American forces in the 20th century. Included in the collection is a life mask of Abraham Lincoln, 19th-century proof engravings of the Battle of Gettysburg, and Vermont uniforms from 1850 to the present. The library contains rosters of Vermonters in all wars, books on Vermont and the Vermont Militia, including the manuscripts of the soon-to-be-published papers of the Vermont National Guard from 1764 on.

FORT WARD MUSEUM

4301 W. Braddock Rd., Alexandria, VA 22304
Telephone: (703) 750-6425
Curator: Cynthia E. Grant
Hours: Tuesday through Saturday 9 A.M. to 5 P.M.;
Sunday noon to 5 P.M.; closed Thanksgiving,
Christmas, and New Year's Day
Cost of admission: Free to the public
Description: The museum's collection of objects reflects military history of the Civil War period. Special collections consist of musical instruments, medical equipment, and personal belongings of military. The strongest representation is in shoulder weapons, particularly carbines, and in Union accouterments. There are revolving interpretive exhibits and a research library. Fort Ward is adjacent to Civil War sites and is the fifth largest of the 68 forts manned to protect the nation's capital during the Civil War.

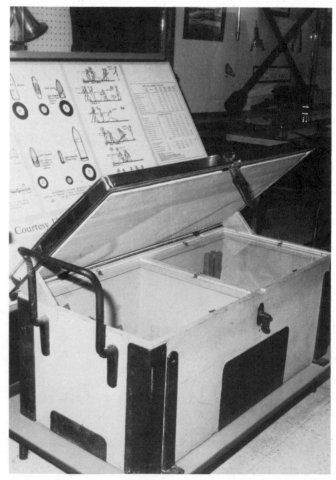

Civil War ammunition box—instructions on how to fire a cannon in background.

APPOMATTOX COURT HOUSE NATIONAL HISTORICAL PARK

P.O. Box 218, Appomattox, VA 24522
Telephone: (804) 352-8987
Superintendent: Luis E. Garcia-Curbelo
Hours: Daily 8:30 A.M. to 5:30 P.M.; closed Christmas
Cost of admission: April through October $1 per vehicle; senior citizens over 62 years free
Description: Appomattox Court House is on Va. 24, 3 miles northeast of the town of the same name. The site was an obscure village when Gen. Robert E. Lee surrendered the Army of Northern Virginia, and was typical of hundreds of hamlets throughout the South. A Union soldier noted at the time that it consisted of only a handful of dwellings, a tavern, and a courthouse. "All on one street and that was boarded up at one end to keep the cows out." There were also law offices, blacksmith shops, stores, and a variety of other buildings. Today the village closely reflects its 1865 appearance.

Appomattox Court House National Historical Park in Virginia, famous as the site of Lee's surrender to Grant in 1865, today is a tranquil rural area that attracts thousands of visitors annually.

U.S. ARMY ENGINEER MUSEUM

16th St. and Belvoir Rd. (Bldg. 1000), Fort Belvoir, VA 22060
Telephone: (703) 664-6104
Curator: Edward B. Russell
Hours: Monday through Friday 8 A.M. to 4:30 P.M.; Saturday 1 P.M. to 4 P.M.; closed federal holidays
Cost of admission: Free to the public
Description: Fort Belvoir is 15 miles south of Washington, D.C. From I-95 take the Belvoir/ Newington exit, proceed east on Backlick Rd. 6 miles to Pohick Gate, Fort Belvoir. Historical holdings of the museum depict the contribution of the Corps of Engineers to the nation over the past 2 centuries. The collection includes military engineering equipment, uniforms, photo-

Display relating history of Army Engineers during the Revolutionary War.

graphs, maps, flags, insignia, and small arms; over 10,000 18th-century artifacts recovered from the site of Belvoir Manor on the post; original maps prepared by French engineers at the siege of Yorktown (1781); the original ship's wheel recovered from the battleship *Maine*, sunk in Havana harbor in 1898; two satellites prepared for the SECOR project (1964); several rare small arms and edged weapons; and over 600 Engineer insignia.

U.S. ARMY TRANSPORTATION MUSEUM

Drawer D, Fort Eustis, VA 23604
Telephone: (804) 878-3603
Curator: Mrs. Emma-Jo L. Davis
Hours: Monday through Friday 8 A.M. to 5 P.M.; Saturday and holidays 10 A.M. to 5 P.M.; Sunday noon to 5 P.M.
Cost of admission: Free to the public
Description: Fort Eustis is 10 miles south of Williamsburg from I-64; take the Fort Eustis exit 1 mile to the main gate. Museum is on Washington Avenue, ½ mile from main gate. Dioramas, exhibits, and art depict the history of

Narrow gauge railroad, U.S. Army Transportation Museum.

Heavy-duty military truck.

Army transportation from the Revolution till today, with projections to the year 2000. The adjoining park displays over 60 vehicles and aircraft including steam locomotives, amphibians, helicopters, fixed-wing aircraft and hovercraft. Exhibits in the museum include an extensive model collection showing various aspects of Army transportation, such as expeditions in the Arctic and the use of Conestoga wagons during the Revolution. The museum also displays paintings, unit flags, insignia, and other memorabilia relating to the history of U.S. Army transportation.

QUARTERMASTER MUSEUM

Fort Lee, VA 23801
Telephone: (804) 734-1854
Director: Henry B. Davis, Jr.
Hours: Monday through Friday 8 A.M. to 5 P.M.; weekends and holidays 11 A.M. to 5 P.M.
Cost of admission: Free to the public
Description: The museum is located on Va. 36, east from Petersburg, just inside the main gate of Fort Lee, on Ave. A. Look for the Fort Lee and Quartermaster Museum signs located on I-85 and I-95 exits near Petersburg. Said to be

One of many life-size displays.

Exterior of Quartermaster Museum, Fort Lee, Va.

one of the most interesting in the entire Army museum system, the museum displays army uniforms, equipment, saddlery, harness, flags, insignia, chevrons, medals, Eisenhower's Command van, Patton's Jeep, Eisenhower's uniforms, Pershing's furniture, Grant's and Pierce's saddles, military subsistence, mortuary exhibits, and "Lady-Be-Good" exhibit; also on display are paintings, prints, and military items too numerous to catalogue. One diorama features a World War I balloon basket, complete with an observer clothed in an authentic uniform of the period. In the museum's Heraldry Room is the only collection of presidential colors in the United States.

CASEMATE MUSEUM

P.O. Box 341, Fort Monroe, VA 23651
Telephone: (804) 727-3391 or 727-3397
Curator: R. Cody Phillips
Hours: Daily 10:30 A.M. to 5 P.M.; closed
Thanksgiving, Christmas, and New Year's Day
Cost of admission: Free to the public

Description: Fort Monroe is across the channel from Norfolk. From the north take I-64 east toward Norfolk. From Norfolk take the same highway going west. Signs mark turnoff. Exhibits cover the history of Fort Monroe, Old Point Comfort, and the U.S. Army Coast Artillery. Several 19th-century artillery weapons; the cell in which Jefferson Davis was imprisoned following the Civil War; Monitor and Merrimac diorama; coast artillery weapons; 2 original Remington paintings, and a reference library (open by appointment only) are a few of the things to be seen. Edgar Allan Poe spent a brief portion of his military career at Fort Monroe, from December 15, 1828, to April 15, 1829. During his enlistment Poe rose from the rank of "artificer" (soldier mechanic) to sergeant major.

Aerial view of Fort Monroe.

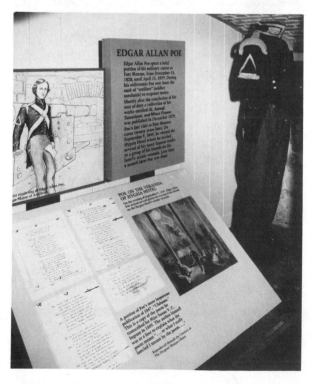

Edgar Allan Poe exhibit at the Casemate Museum.

Interior of the Fort Monroe Casemate Museum.

Living quarters exhibit.

OLD GUARD MUSEUM

3rd U.S. Infantry, Fort Myer, VA 22211
Telephone: (202) 692-9721
Curator: Charles R. R. Vassar
Hours: Monday through Saturday 10 A.M. to 4
P.M.; closed holidays
Cost of admission: Free to the public

Description: The museum features shoulder-fired weapons from 1775 to present, as well as bayonets from 1775 and other appendages. It contains one of this nation's most complete Infantry crest collections, uniforms from 1784 to the present, flags from 1776, and headgear from 1789 to present. Other diverse items include an 18th-century brass spitoon with its own story, sabers and swords from 1840 to 1914, a presidential baton presented to the 3rd Infantry by Harry Truman, 11 works of art from the U.S. Army Art Collection, gas masks from World War I; canteens from 1860; a diorama of the 3rd Cavalry worth $14,000, munitions from 1860 to 1950, and edged weapons from the Philippines of 1800–1900. A large reference library from 1840 is open to visitors. The 3rd

Entrance to museum building, which faces on the parade ground.

Infantry, called The Old Guard, also maintains a faithful 24-hour vigil at the Tomb of the Unknown Soldier. They render military honors for funerals in adjacent Arlington National Cemetery and participate in state funerals.

Honor Guard on parade, full-dress blues, at Fort Myer.

Display case devoted to Gen. John J. Pershing's famed horse Black Jack.

After serving a tour of duty with the honor guard, a soldier is entitled to wear this metal badge on his uniform.

FREDERICKSBURG AND SPOTSYLVANIA NATIONAL MILITARY PARK

P.O. Box 679, Fredericksburg, VA 22401

Telephone: (703) 373-4461

Superintendent: Dixon B. Freeland

Hours: Daily 9 A.M. to 5 P.M.; closed Christmas and New Year's Day

Cost of admission: Free to the public

Description: This military park commemorates the following Civil War actions: Battle of Fredericksburg, December 11–13, 1862; Chancellorsville Campaign (Chancellorsville, Second

Fredericksburg and Spotsylvania National Military Park, where living history is portrayed.

"Fire!" A pull of the lanyard and the mortar goes off. During the summer the solid plaster projectiles never once hit the target, a red flag. But they consistently landed close enough so that the shell burst; had the projectile been an original one, it would have destroyed the target.

Union artifacts.

Exhibit showing Confederate artifacts.

Fredericksburg, and Salem Church), April 27–May 6, 1863; Battle of the Wilderness, May 5–6, 1864; Battle of Spotsylvania Court House, May 8–21, 1864. This park contains 5,644 acres dispersed over 7 major locations. The Fredericksburg Visitor Center/Museum has a 15-minute sound/slide program and 2 floors of exhibits; Chancellorsville visitor center has a 12-minute sound/slide program and exhibits; Jackson Shrine is the historic house where Stonewall Jackson died; Chatham is the 18th-century mansion and Civil War headquarters. A self-guided tour of all 4 battlefields and 3 historic buildings begins at the Fredericksburg Battlefield Visitor Center on U.S. 1, Lafayette Blvd.

WARREN RIFLES CONFEDERATE MUSEUM

95 Chester St., Front Royal, VA 22630
Telephone: (703) 636-9068
President-Trustee: Miss Virginia Hale
Hours: Monday through Saturday 9 A.M. to 6 P.M.;
Sunday 1 P.M. to 6 P.M.
Cost of admission: Adults $1; children under 12
years free
Description: The museum is devoted to relics and records of War between the States. These include arms, battle flags, uniforms and accouterments, cavalry equipment, rare documents, and pictures, personal and domestic items and memorabilia of Belle Boyd, Mosby's Rangers, Generals Jackson, Lee, Early, Longstreet, Ashby, et al. A collection of sabers, guns, belt buckles, cartridge boxes, uniform buttons, uniforms, and other items is also on display.

A local youngster proudly shows the way to the Warren Rifles Confederate Museum.

A unique miniature shrine made of sea shells, backed by Confederate flag.

GEORGE C. MARSHALL LIBRARY AND MUSEUM

Drawer 920, Lexington, VA 24450
Telephone: (703) 463-7103
Director: Fred L. Hadsel
Hours: Monday through Saturday 9 A.M. to 5 P.M.;
October 15 through April 15 9 A.M. to 4 P.M.;
Sunday 2 P.M. to 5 P.M.
Cost of admission: Free to the public
Description: The museum in the Marshall Library

highlights the contributions made by Gen. George C. Marshall during his long and distinguished career of public service. The many associations he formed with world leaders while gaining their universal respect as a global strategist and statesman are vividly illustrated by the artifacts, photographs, and documents. Special educational programs using the library's museum and archival collection are also available by appointment for visiting grade school and high school groups. Arrangements must be made in advance by writing or by telephone.

Interior view of the George C. Marshall Research Library, Virginia Military Institute at Lexington, Ky.

George C. Marshall museum lobby.

VIRGINIA MILITARY INSTITUTE MUSEUM

Jackson Memorial Hall, Lexington, VA 24450
Telephone: (703) 463-6232
Curator: Mrs. June Cunningham
Hours: Monday through Friday 9 A.M. to 4:30
P.M.; Saturday 9 A.M. to 5 P.M.; Sundays and
holidays noon to 5 P.M.; closed from Christmas to
New Year's Day
Cost of admission: Free to the public

Description: The VMI Museum tells numerous stories. It relates the development of the Virginia Military Institute from its founding in 1839, the story of the VMI Corps of Cadets, and the story of dedicated service to the nation in times of peace and war by VMI alumni. The museum has existed as an "organized" collection of historic artifacts since 1908, although the collection was probably begun in 1875 when Benjamin Brinker presented to the Institute the sword carried by Gen. Richard Montgomery in the Battle of Quebec in 1775. During the course of its history, this museum has been located in the VMI barracks, the old Smith Building, the old library, Nichols Engineering Hall, Preston Library, and, since 1968, in Jackson Memorial Hall. The museum possesses a large Civil War collection, including such items as Jackson's favorite kepi and the raincoat he wore on the night of his fatal shooting.

Panels explaining the charge of the VMI cadets.

Stonewall Jackson's personal belongings.

MANASSAS NATIONAL BATTLEFIELD PARK

P.O. Box 1830, Manassas, VA 22110
Telephone: (703) 754-7107
Historian: Stuart G. Vogt
Hours: Daily 9 A.M. to 6:30 P.M.; closed Christmas
Cost of admission: Free to the public

Description: Manassas National Battlefield Park is 26 miles southwest of Washington, D.C., near the intersection of I-66 and Va. 234. The visitor center offers a museum, slide program, and battle map. Here are housed documents and artifacts relating to campaigns and battles of the First and Second Manassas. There is also a research library open to scholars upon written request. Included in this library are the papers of two Union generals, James Brewerton Ricketts and Fitz-John Porter. The First Manassas had its beginning on July 21, 1861. The deep-throated roar of a 30-pounder Parrott rifle shattered the morning calm where Stone Bridge carried the Warrenton Turnpike across Bull Run. Soon the smaller cannons added their bark to the din. Men on both sides of the stream waited, one group to attack, the other to defend. Now there would be no turning back; the battle, and then the war, would be fought to the bitter end.

Gen. Joseph E. Johnson in command of the Army of the Shenandoah.

Maj. Gen. Beauregard on the battlefield at Bull Run, Sunday, July 21, 1861.

197

Reenactment of the First Battle of Manassas on July 21, 1961.

NEW MARKET BATTLEFIELD AND HALL OF VALOR

P.O. Box 1864, New Market, VA 22844

Telephone: (703) 740-3101

Director: James J. Geary

Hours: Daily 9 A.M. to 5 P.M.; closed Christmas

Cost of admission: Adults $1.75; children 75¢

Description: The Hall of Valor features two award-winning motion pictures on the Civil War in the Shenandoah Valley, one on the Battle of New Market in which Virginia Military Institute cadets created a legend of valor, and the other on the war in the valley as a whole, especially Stonewall Jackson's Valley Campaign of 1862. Exhibits in the 2-story Virginia Room trace in chronological order all the major campaigns in Virginia; and there are generalized exhibits on statistics, new inventions, the use of railroads, and artillery. The 160-acre park includes the restored Bushong farm that was overrun in the Battle of New Market.

Young, previously untested cadets of Virginia Military Institute, in a unique incident in American history, swarmed around this picturesque old farmhouse under heavy fire and went on to capture a cannon and many prisoners in the 1864 Battle of New Market. Known as the Bushong house, it is now part of the 160-acre New Market Battlefield Park, which lies on a rolling hill in the heart of the Shenandoah Valley. The Hall of Valor serves the park as a visitor center and as a memorial to the cadets.

WAR MEMORIAL MUSEUM OF VIRGINIA

9285 Warwick Blvd., Huntington Park, Newport News, VA 23607
Telephone: (804) 247-8523
Curator: John V. Quarstein
Hours: Monday through Saturday 9 A.M. to 5 P.M.; Sunday 1 P.M. to 5 P.M.; closed Christmas and New Year's Day
Cost of admission: Adults 50¢; military, children, and senior citizens 25¢

Description: A comprehensive display of over 20,000 artifacts, including weapons, uniforms, vehicles, posters, insignia, and accouterments relating to every major U.S. military involvement. Exhibit areas include: 20th-century military uniforms of the world; U.S. military history, 1776 to present; the Axis Powers; World War II; evolution of weapons; and insignias of the world. There is also a military history library and film collection, with weekend film programs. The museum is located in Huntington Park, which overlooks the James River, with picnic areas and recreational facilities available for visitors.

The U.S. Shipping Board produced this poster (c. 1918) to encourage production during World War I.

Much of the Civil War is surveyed in the 2-story Virginia Room of the New Market Battlefield's museum, the Hall of Valor, with this life-size centerpiece commanding the lower level. On the upper mezzanine, exhibits relate in chronological order the massive campaigns of the "on-to-Richmond" strategy of the Union high command.

A World War II poster (c. 1942) produced by the U.S. Government Printing Office.

GENERAL DOUGLAS MACARTHUR MEMORIAL MUSEUM

MacArthur Square, Norfolk, VA 23510
Telephone: (804) 441-2382 or 441-2256
Director: Lyman H. Hammond, Jr.
Hours: Daily 10 A.M. to 5 P.M.; November to
March, Tuesday through Sunday; closed
Thanksgiving, Christmas, and New Year's Day
Cost of admission: Free to the public

Description: There are a total of 9 galleries. Number 1 contains the first of 6 murals representing the general's life. Number 2 holds displays from the Philippines. Number 3 is dedicated to France and World War I. Number 4 covers World War II. Number 5 comprises the general's collection of canes, pipes, and Japanese swords. Number 6 is the "surrender" room and holds mementos of the day that ended World War II. Number 7 commemorates the Korean War. Number 8 holds medals, badges, and swords given to the general. Number 9 treats his days after returning to the U.S. MacArthur Archives and Library are also part of this museum. The general's personal files and those of his staff, as well as his 4,000-volume library, are housed here. Most of the 690 feet of correspondence, reports, messages, photographs, newspaper files, and scrapbooks are declassified and are constantly in use by researchers interested in military history and the occupation of Japan.

Statue of Douglas MacArthur outside Gen. Douglas MacArthur Memorial Museum.

A montage of events in General MacArthur's life.

PETERSBURG NATIONAL BATTLEFIELD

Petersburg Nat'l Battlefield, P.O. Box 549,
Petersburg, VA 23803
Telephone: (804) 732-3531
Superintendent: Wallace B. Elms
Hours: Visitor center museum, daily 8 A.M. to 5
P.M.

Cost of admission: Free to the public

Description: The park visitor center and its museum are off Va. 36, just outside of Petersburg. Their emphasis is on the siege of Petersburg, June 1864 to April 1865. A 20-minute map show offers an overview of troop locations and major troop movements. Grounds encompass 4 miles of siege lines including areas of the opening battles of the siege, battle of the crater, and battle of Fort Stedman. In a grim 10-month struggle Ulysses S. Grant's Union Army gradually but relentlessly encircled Petersburg and cut Robert E. Lee's railroad supply lines from the south. For the Confederates it was 10 months of desperately hanging on, hoping the people of the North would tire of the war. For soldiers of both armies it was a period of rifle bullets, artillery, and mortar shells. Added to the danger were drill and more drill, plus salt pork and cornmeal, burned beans, and bad coffee.

Interior view of the visitor center and museum at Petersburg National Battlefield.

Battery 5, 1864.

Battery 5. Strongest Confederate work on their original line. It was captured on the first day of the opening battle. A trail leads to a replica of "The Dictator," the huge Union mortar used to shell Petersburg.

Living history exhibit.

MUSEUM OF THE CONFEDERACY

1201 E. Clay St., Richmond, VA 23219
Telephone: (804) 649-1861
Curator: Dr. Edward D. C. Campbell, Jr.
*Hours: Monday through Saturday 10 A.M. to 5
P.M.; Sunday 2 P.M. to 5 P.M.; closed major
holidays*
Cost of admission: Adults $1; children 50¢
Description: The Museum of the Confederacy
holds the material remains of the Confederate
States of America. These remains have been
carefully preserved and consist of everything
from paintings, firearms, personal military equipage, and battle remnants to lady's handstitch-
ing. The Confederacy was born in times of strife
and expired in the same fashion. This museum
tells it all.

Picture in 1865 of the building that now serves as the
Museum of the Confederacy, Richmond, Va.

Confederate railroad supply depot, Savage Station, Va.

RICHMOND NATIONAL BATTLEFIELD PARK

3215 E. Broad St., Richmond, VA 23223
Telephone: (804) 226-1981
Superintendent: Sylvester Putman
Hours: Daily 9 A.M. to 5 P.M.; closed Christmas and New Year's Day

Cost of admission: Free to the public

Description: A complete tour of the battlefields, which includes those of 1862 and 1864, requires a 97-mile drive as outlined on a map presented to each visitor. There are several visitor center/museums along the way. Also presented is a show of "living history." This is an interpretive technique used in many national parks, which offers visitors the opportunity to see a part of the museum's story, as well as hear about it. It

Chimborayo Visitor Center and Museum, Richmond National Battlefield Park.

Height of typical Civil War battle which took place around Richmond, Va.

supplies a person with whom visitors can identify, with whom they can talk, and from whom they can learn about day-to-day life of a past era. From that touchstone, the visitors can go on to learn more from the park's exhibits, audiovisual program, and publications. There is much to see here, as the struggle for Richmond preoccupied Northerner and Southerner alike for 4 years. If the South lost its capital, Southerners might lose their will to fight—so reasoned leaders on both sides in the early years of the war. There were other reasons as well, for Richmond was a medical and manufacturing center, and the supply depot for troops of the Confederacy.

COLONIAL NATIONAL HISTORICAL PARK, YORKTOWN VISITOR CENTER

P.O. Box 210, Yorktown, VA 23690
Telephone: (804) 898-3400

Superintendent: James R. Sullivan
Hours: Daily 8:30 A.M. to 6:00 P.M.; closed Christmas
Cost of admission: Free to the public
Description: This park includes Jamestown, Yorktown Battlefield, Colonial Parkway, and Cape Henry Memorial. The visitor center/museum has an orientation map with narration; a 12-minute film, *Surrender at Yorktown,* shown

This diorama in the National Park Service's Yorktown Visitor Center depicts Gen. George Washington firing the first gun at the Siege of Yorktown in 1781. On October 19, the surrender of Lord Cornwallis's British army to the combined French and American forces virtually ensured the success of the Americans' War for Independence.

every 30 minutes; and exhibits that include a full-size replica of a portion of the British frigate *Charon;* tents used by George Washington at the siege of Yorktown; dioramas, and Revolutionary War artifacts and cannons. In August 1781—with the Revolutionary War in its seventh year—General Washington received word that a large French fleet commanded by the Comte de Grasse would arrive soon in Virginia. After conferring with General Rochambeau, Washington began secretly to move the bulk of his forces from their camps in New York toward Virginia. He hoped that Cornwallis's army would still be there when he arrived. Cornwallis was dismayed when the French fleet blockaded Chesapeake Bay and on September 5 defeated a British fleet attempting to break the blockade. This was the beginning of the end for the British.

Historic markers along the trail of the Yorktown Park.

FORT CHRISTIANSVAERN

P.O. Box 160, Christiansted,
St. Croix, Virgin Islands 00820
Hours: Monday through Saturday 8 A.M. to 4:30
P.M.
Cost of admission: Free to the public
Description: Fort Christiansvaern, in downtown Christiansted, is the best preserved of the 5 remaining Danish forts in the Virgin Islands. Largely completed by 1749, the Danish army garrisoned there until 1878, when it became a police station and courthouse. The fort was built mainly of hard yellow bricks brought from Denmark as ballast in sailing ships, and although numerous minor additions and alterations have since been made, its appearance remains relatively unchanged. It is a prime example of 17th- and 18th-century Danish colonial military architecture.

Courtyard, Fort Christiansvaern, Christiansted National Historic Site.

FORT COLUMBIA

P.O. Box 236, Chinook, WA 98614
Telephone: (206) 777-8221
State Park Manager: Terry Carlson
Hours: Summer, Wednesday through Sunday 9 A.M.
to 5 P.M.; winter 10 A.M. to 3 P.M.
Cost of admission: Free to the public

Description: The first work for Fort Columbia, which is located at Chinook Point, was the construction of an 8-inch battery. Together with a harbor mining casemate, it was completed in 1898. Later other batteries were added. The fort was completed in 1902. The former enlisted men's barracks is now an interpretive center (museum) which tells the story of the U.S. Coast Artillery. The former commandant's quarters now houses a museum sponsored by the local chapter of the Daughters of the American Revolution (DAR). The former administration building operates as an art gallery, featuring the work of local artists. The former hospital operates as a youth hostel (AYH approved).

Fort Columbia, Interpretive Center Barracks.

FORT CASEY COASTAL DEFENSE HERITAGE SITE

1280 S. Fort Casey Rd., Coupeville, WA 98239
Telephone: (206) 678-4519
Hours: Varying hours
Cost of admission: Free to the public

Description: Fort Casey was one of the coast artillery posts established during the late 1890s for the defense of Puget Sound. Together with the heavy batteries of Fort Worden and Fort Flagler, its guns guarded the entrance to Admiralty Inlet, the key point in the fortification system designed to prevent a hostile fleet from reaching such prime targets as the Bremerton Navy Yard and the cities of Seattle, Tacoma, Olympia, and Everett. Large guns mounted on disappearing carriages were a characteristic feature of early coastal forts. Guns of this type were withdrawn behind a thick concrete parapet after each round was fired. The Washington State

Fort Casey, 10-inch gun emplacement.

Parks and Recreation Commission acquired Fort Casey in 1956 and initiated an interpretive program to provide the public with a complete story of an example of coast artillery. An interpretive center explaining coastal defense forts has been installed in one section of the site. Two 3-inch rapid-fire guns and two 10-inch disappearing carriage guns have been procured from Fort Wint in the Philippines and are on display.

FORT SPOKANE VISITOR CENTER

Coulee Dam National Recreation Center, Star Rt., Box 30, Davenport, WA 99122
Telephone: (509) 725-2715
Curator: District Ranger
Hours: Daily, mid-June to Labor Day 8 A.M. to 6 P.M.
Cost of admission: Free to the public
Description: Military displays and diagrams with artifacts over the 1880–96 period of history for Fort Spokane are depicted. Photographic displays and audiovisual presentations are also available for viewing. A 1-mile self-guided trail leads from visitor center museum and tours grounds of the fort. Because of warring Indians, this fort was built in 1880 at the confluence of the Columbia and Spokane rivers. Combined with expanding telegraph, railroad, and trail systems, this location offered protection for the communities to the south, the settlers in the Colville and Okanogan valleys, and conflicting Indian tribes throughout the district.

Guardhouse constructed in 1892 at Fort Spokane, now used as a visitor center. Living history programs are presented on Sundays.

FORT LEWIS MILITARY MUSEUM

Bldg. 4320, Fort Lewis, WA 98433

Telephone: (206) 967-5524 or 967-4796

Curator: Barbara A. Dierking

Hours: Daily noon to 4 P.M.; closed major holidays

Cost of admission: Free to the public

Description: Fort Lewis is 20 miles east of Olympia, Wash. The museum maintains 3 separate historical collections totaling over 6,000 items and deals with 4 major areas: the 9th Infantry Division; the 6th Infantry Division; Fort Lewis history; and outdoor displays of military vehicles and artillery. In addition, the museum has approximately 7,000 photographs and 3,000 research books and documents in its archives. Exhibits also include souvenirs of overseas assignments; uniforms, equipment, and weapons of allies and enemies of the 4 major conflicts since 1917; and specialized displays of awards and decorations, shoulder patches, distinctive insignia, colors and guidons of units. A 1½-acre outside display park shows vehicles, tanks, missiles, and artillery.

World War II mounted officers' den exhibit at Fort Lewis Military Museum.

LEWIS AND CLARK INTERPRETIVE CENTER

Fort Canby State Park, P.O. Box 108, Ilwaco, WA 98624

Telephone: (206) 642-3029

Interpretive Assistant: George Eidson

Cost of admission: Free to the public

Description: The center is primarily concerned with the Lewis and Clark Expedition. The journey is depicted through wall displays, audiovisual presentations, and artifacts exhibits. Quotes from the original journals of the expedition give the visitor an idea of the moods and feelings of the men. On the upper display floor are exhibits about shipwrecks, the U.S. Coast Guard, and the military features of Fort Canby and the Coast Artillery. A slide show depicts the history of the fort, and a cannonball and portion of a disappearing gun carriage found at the park are on display. From his perch on the cliff high above the surf, the visitor can look out over the mouth of the Columbia River and Pacific Ocean, which gives some idea why the fort was built—to guard the entrance of the river. The library (open by appointment) also contains an extensive collection of military artifacts and army manuals on coast artillery, as well as a large number of blueprints, charts, and maps of the fort. The center (museum) is built adjacent to a gun battery that was active through World War II.

The Lewis and Clark Interpretive Center at Fort Canby State Park, Washington.

SCHIFFNER MILITARY MUSEUM

Star Rt., Box 193, Moses Lake, WA 98837
Telephone: (509) 765-6374
Curator: George Schiffner
Hours: By appointment
Cost of admission: Donations only
Description: The collection consists of materials from all the services: uniforms, field equipment, personal military belongings, a patch collection, medals, medical equipment used in the field, personal items belonging to military personnel donated to the museum, and a reference library.

Air Force dress whites and service blues.

FORT FLAGLER

Port Townsend, WA 98368
Address inquiries to: Washington Parks and
Recreation Commission, Interpretive Services, P.O.
Box 1128, Olympia, WA 98501
Cost of admission: Free to the public

Description: In 1884 a board of officers, appointed by Gen. Nelson A. Miles, recommended that the defense of Puget Sound should rely upon batteries of 10-inch guns and large mortars on Marrowstone Point, Point Wilson, and Admiralty Head at the entrance to the Admiralty Inlet. For a number of years this triangle defense was not recognized by the military even though later developments in ordnance made it possible to set up this line of defense. With the establishment in 1891 at Bremerton of the Puget Sound Navy Yard, there was concern for its protection. On June 6, 1896, an act of Congress authorized the expenditure of funds for construction of heavy gun emplacements at Marrowstone Point, Point Wilson, and Admiralty Head. Although the guns at Fort Flagler were never fired at a hostile target, this fortification remains a good example of a type of strategy that was important to the U.S. before the advent of the airplane and nuclear weapons.

Fort Flagler, 3-inch rapid-fire gun.

FORT WORDEN COAST ARTILLERY MUSEUM

P.O. Box 499, Port Townsend, WA 98368
Telephone: (206) 385-4730, Ext. 34
Director: Col. Stan Lilian, ARNG (Ret.)

Hours: Monday through Friday 9 A.M. to 5 P.M.;
weekends and holidays noon to 6 P.M.
Cost of admission: Free to the public

Description: This museum is devoted to harbor defense and the Coast Artillery (1910–53), and shows how personnel lived, how the various types of armament were operated, the military method of plotting and position finding, and the scheme of harbor defenses for Puget Sound. Its displays include a collection of armaments (3-inch to 16-inch guns, 12-inch mortars), dioramas, models, tapes, slides, and motion pictures, artifacts, and photos. Five forts are depicted: Worden (headquarters), Casey, Ebey, Flagler, and (Camp) Hayden, plus other miscellaneous batteries and fortifications from 1890 to 1944.

OLD FORT TOWNSEND

Rt. 1, Port Townsend, WA 98368

Cost of admission: Free to the public

Description: Indian uprisings in the 1850s caused the people of Port Townsend, a prosperous port of entry on Puget Sound, to ask the U.S. Army for protection. In 1856, Maj. Granville O. Haller was ordered by the War Department to proceed with Company I, 4th Infantry, to establish a post on Port Townsend Bay. This site, 3 miles south of Port Townsend, was selected. Gen. William Harney inspected Fort Townsend in 1859 and immediately ordered its evacuation. The fort was under caretaker status until 1874 when it was reactivated. In 1895, fire destroyed the barracks and the post was abandoned. A display shelter serves as a museum and interprets the story of this early fort.

Soldiers in front of flagpole at Old Fort Townsend.

MUSEUM OF HISTORY AND INDUSTRY

2161 E. Hamlin St., Seattle, WA 98112
Telephone: (206) 324-1125
Curator: William Stannard
Hours: Monday through Friday 11 A.M. to 5 P.M.;
Saturday 10 A.M. to 5 P.M.; closed holidays
Cost of admission: Free to the public

Description: The museum features material relating to Pacific Northwest history, especially Seattle and King County. Additional collections of military significance include the Goodspeed Collection of ethnographic weapons, representing edged weapons and firearms from around the world. The museum also contains a complete collection of military uniforms from Civil War through Vietnam and a large photograph collection (approximately 75,000 negatives) on local and national themes, along with paper ephemera from roughly 1850 to the present.

Museum of History and Industry.

FORT GEORGE WRIGHT HISTORICAL MUSEUM

W. 4000 Randolph Rd., Spokane, WA 99204
Telephone: (509) 328-2970, Ext. 38
Curator: Trudie Nesbitt
Hours: By appointment: (509) 487-8270; closed holidays

Cost of admission: Donations only
Description: The museum is housed in a 3-story turn-of-the-century army officer's home. The house has been completely restored, with a pre-electric area kitchen that is often used for living history demonstrations. The museum was founded to preserve the story of Fort George Wright, the men who served there, the families who lived there, and its impact on Spokane. In addition to its large military collection, the museum has a doll room containing over 300 antique dolls and toys and a reference library

featuring letters and documents from the Mexican War to 1958, at which time the fort was deactivated. Although the museum is on a college campus, it does not belong to the college. It is maintained by a community nonprofit organization that runs on donations, and is staffed mainly by volunteers.

Fort George Wright Historical Museum.

FORT NISQUALLY MUSEUM

Point Defiance Park, Tacoma, WA 98407
Telephone: (206) 759-1246
Curator: Steven A. Anderson
Hours: Wednesday through Friday 10 A.M. to 6
P.M.; weekends and holidays 11 A.M. to 6 P.M.
Cost of admission: Free to the public
Description: The outdoor museum contains the oldest standing building in the state of Washington—the granary, dating from 1843. The fort also consists of a stockade, two blockhouses, a blacksmith shop, a fur trading store, a laundry, a bakery, and a replica of Nisqually House (first settlement on Puget Sound). Within the fort, many of the buildings contain period tools, furniture, and artifacts. The museum building contains antiques dating from 1840 and an entire section for Northwestern Indian artifacts and beadwork. Frontier items, such as early frontier rifles, an Indian handmade canoe, pioneer sewing machines, organs, pianos, and implements are all on display. Fort Nisqually was originally built in 1833.

The porch of the Fort Nisqually Museum.

Northeast bastion.

SAN JUAN ISLAND

P.O. Box 549, Friday Harbor, WA 98250
Address inquiries to: Superintendent, 300
Cattlepoint Rd., Friday Harbor, WA 98250
Cost of admission: Free to the public
Description: San Juan Island is reached by Washington State ferries from Anacortes, Wash., which is 83 miles north of Seattle. An interpretive shelter near the park headquarters contains an exhibit describing the background of the American-British boundary dispute. A historic trail leads from the shelter area across the American campsite to the redoubt and returns via the site of Bellevue Farm, the successful sheep ranch once owned by the Hudson's Bay Co.

English camp, San Juan Island.

FORT VANCOUVER

E. Evergreen Blvd., Vancouver, WA 98661

Cost of admission: Free to the public

Description: To visit the park, turn east off I-5 at the Mill Plain Blvd. interchange and then follow the signs to the visitor center. Founded by the Hudson's Bay Co. during the winter of 1824–25 as a fur trading post and supply depot, Fort Vancouver for the next 20 years was the most important settlement in the Pacific Northwest, from San Francisco Bay to the Russian outposts in Alaska. The early 1800s saw England, America, Spain, and Russia competing for control of the Northwest fur trade. Russia and Spain soon limited their claims. In 1818 the United States and England agreed to share access to the Oregon country until a boundary could be drawn. Seven years later the Hudson's Bay Co. moved its headquarters from Fort George at the mouth of the Columbia and founded Fort Vancouver 100 miles upstream. It was a bold move designed to anchor Britain's claim on Oregon. Five years later the fort was moved closer to the river.

Entrance sign at Fort Vancouver.

Army house built in 1849, officers' row along parade ground, Vancouver Barracks.

FORT SIMCOE STATE PARK HERITAGE SITE

Fort Rd., White Swan, WA 98952
Cost of admission: Free to the public
Description: Fort Simcoe was one of 2 regular Army posts established in the interior of Washington Territory as a consequence of Indian hostilities beginning in the fall of 1855. The site now consists of 200 acres located at the western end of Wash. 220. Of the military structures that framed the 420-foot-square parade ground, 5 remain: the commanding officer's handsome house, 3 trim dwellings that were captains' quarters, and a squared log blockhouse on a slight elevation at the southwest approach. A brick museum displays, in addition to military artifacts, Indian craftwork and other exhibits depicting the story of this fort and its region.

Commandant's house at Fort Simcoe.

HARPERS FERRY NATIONAL HISTORICAL PARK

Harpers Ferry, WV 25425
Telephone: (304) 535-6371
Superintendent: Donald W. Campbell
Hours: Daily 8 A.M. to 5 P.M.; closed Christmas and New Year's Day
Cost of admission: Free to the public
Description: Harpers Ferry, situated on a point of land at the confluence of the Shenandoah and Potomac rivers and dominated by the Blue Ridge Mountains, was a beckoning wilderness in the early 1700s. By the mid-19th century it was a town of some 3,000 inhabitants, an important arms-producing center, and a transportation

link between east and west. John Brown's raid in 1859 and the Civil War thrust the town into national prominence. The destruction wrought by the war and repeated flooding were responsible for the town's eventual decline. Harpers Ferry Historical Park continues to undergo extensive restoration. As work on additional buildings is completed, the park will expand its program of living history demonstrations, exhibits, and audiovisual presentations.

Otis Company, 22nd New York Infantry at Maryland Heights, Harpers Ferry.

Harpers Ferry as it appears today.

Restored arsenal building.

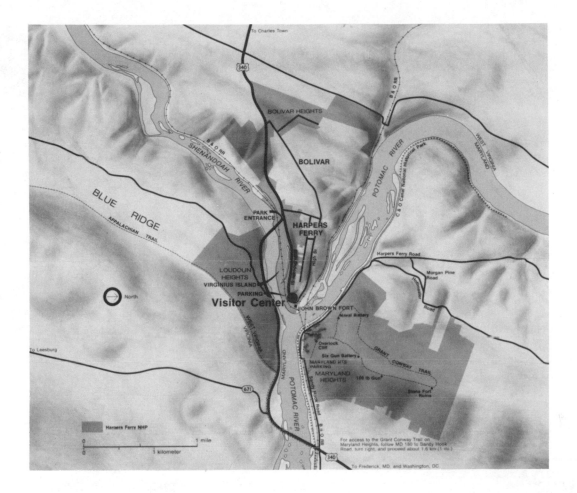

WISCONSIN VETERANS MUSEUM

Marden Memorial Center, King WI 54946
Telephone: (608) 266-1680
Curator: Dr. Richard H. Zeitlin
Hours: Daily 9 A.M. to 11 A.M.; 1 P.M. to 4 P.M.
Cost of admission: Free to the public
Description: The museum focuses on Wisconsin in the world wars. Its collection comprises artifacts, uniforms, posters, flags, maps, equipment, and weapons from World War I and World War II. Displays include uniformed figures and a life-size trench-scene diorama, housed in a modern facility with track lighting. The museum was awarded a 1975 Certificate of Merit from the American Association of State and Local History, and is accredited by the American Association of Museums.

Life-size replica of World War I trench, Wisconsin Veterans Museum.

G.A.R. MEMORIAL HALL MUSEUM

Capitol 419 N., Madison, WI 53702
Telephone: (608) 266-1680
Curator: Dr. Richard H. Zeitlin
Hours: Daily 9 A.M. to 4:30 P.M.; closed holidays
Cost of admission: Free to the public
Description: The museum houses a collection of artifacts, battle flags, weapons, posters, photographs, paintings, equipment, edged weapons, maps, firearms, uniformed figures, and a diorama focusing on Wisconsin's role in the Civil War and Spanish-American War. Housed in landmark G.A.R. Memorial Hall in the State Capitol Building, it also maintains a specialized research library and modest collection of archival materials. G.A.R. Memorial Hall Museum has been accredited by the American Association of Museums.

Display at G.A.R. Memorial Hall Museum.

FORT WINNEBAGO SURGEON'S QUARTERS

Rt. 1, Box 10, Portage, WI 53901
Telephone: (608) 742-2949
Curator: Mrs. Edward J. Schickel
Hours: Daily, May through October 9 A.M. to 5 P.M.
Cost of admission: Adults $2; children (6 to 14 years) 50¢; special group rates
Description: Built in 1824, purchased by the army in 1828, this structure was used as Surgeon's Home until 1845. Museum contains Civil War surgical instruments, early medical books, period furniture, and artifacts of Fort Winnebago. It is the only remaining building of Fort Winnebago. Museum and building are owned by Wisconsin Daughters of the American Revolution.

Surgeon's Quarters and museum, only remaining building of Fort Winnebago.

FORT FETTERMAN STATE MUSEUM

Douglas, WY 82633
Telephone: (307) 358-2864
Hours: 9 A.M. to 6 P.M.; closed during winter
months
Cost of admission: Free to the public
Description: Fort Fetterman, located approx-imately 11 miles southwest of Douglas, Wyo., is situated on a plateau above LaPrele Creek and the North Platte River. It was established as a military post on July 19, 1867, because of conditions on the northern plains at the close of the Civil War. Civilization was advancing across the frontier along the line of the Union Pacific Railroad. The fort was needed as a major supply point for the army operating against the Indians.

General Crook's headquarters, Fort Fetterman.

FORT BRIDGER STATE MUSEUM

Fort Bridger, WY 82933
Telephone: (307) 782-3842
Curator: Tom Lindmier
Hours: Daily, April 15 to May 30 9 A.M. to 5 P.M.;
June 1 to August 20 8 A.M. to 6 P.M.; August 21 to
September 15 8 A.M. to 5 P.M.; September 16 to
October 15 9 A.M. to 5 P.M.; weekends, October 16
to April 14 10 A.M. to 4 P.M.
Cost of admission: Free to the public
Description: The army began work on this fort in spring 1858, first building against the "Mormon Wall" and later expanding to other locations. By 1859 a total of 29 buildings had been constructed. In honor of his friend and former scout, Colonel Johnson, commander of the new post, named it Fort Bridger. With the outbreak of the Civil War, military personnel at Fort Bridger were ordered east. W. A. Carter, a post sutler, organized a volunteer militia of citizens and mountain men for protection. Early in April 1866, a company of "galvanized Yankees" (former Confederate prisoners of war who were allowed to serve in the Union Army on the western frontier rather than remain in prison), were sent to garrison Fort Bridger.

FORT LARAMIE NATIONAL HISTORIC SITE

P.O. Box 178, Fort Laramie, WY 82212
Telephone: (307) 837-2221
Supervisory Historian: Michael C. Livingston
Hours: Daily 8 A.M. to 4:30 P.M.; Memorial Day to Labor Day 8 A.M. to 8 P.M.; closed Christmas and New Year's Day
Cost of admission: Free to the public

Description: The museum deals with the national significance of Fort Laramie from 1834 to 1849. Situated on the eastern Wyoming prairies, it was a fur trading post from 1849 to 1890. It figured prominently in the covered-wagon migrations to Oregon and California, in a series of bloody Indian campaigns, and in many other pioneer events. Artifacts displayed are primarily U.S. Army weaponry and accouterments of the 1870s. Museum photographs depict the various civilian, military, and Indian personalities associated with Fort Laramie's history and its bloody evolution.

Officers' row at Fort Laramie.

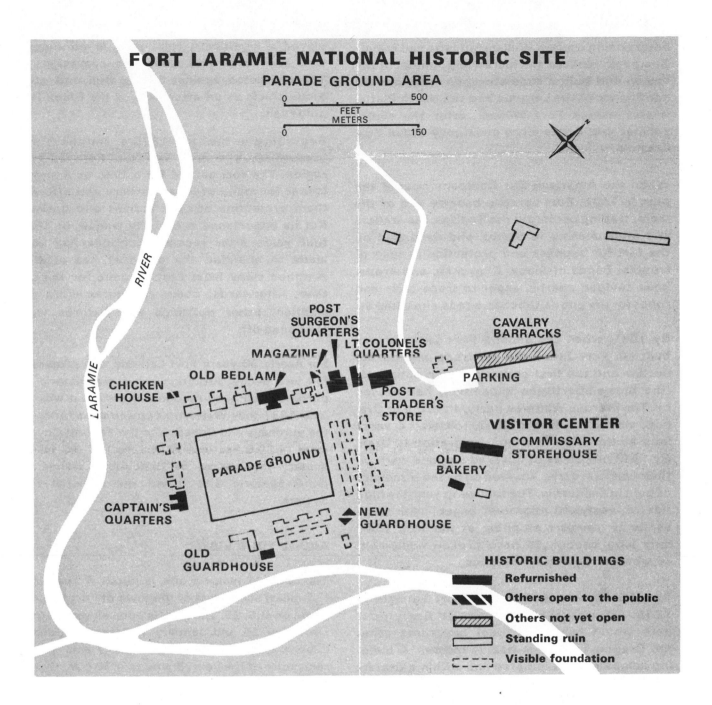

FORT LARAMIE NATIONAL HISTORIC SITE
PARADE GROUND AREA

LARAMIE RIVER

POST SURGEON'S QUARTERS

MAGAZINE

LT COLONEL'S QUARTERS

CAVALRY BARRACKS

OLD BEDLAM

CHICKEN HOUSE

PARKING

POST TRADER'S STORE

VISITOR CENTER

COMMISSARY STOREHOUSE

OLD BAKERY

PARADE GROUND

CAPTAIN'S QUARTERS

NEW GUARDHOUSE

OLD GUARDHOUSE

HISTORIC BUILDINGS

Refurnished

Others open to the public

Others not yet open

Standing ruin

Visible foundation

Part II

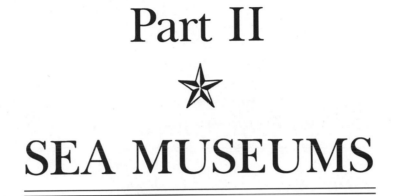

SEA MUSEUMS

USS *ALABAMA* BATTLESHIP MEMORIAL PARK

P.O. Box 65, Battleship Pkwy., Mobile, AL 36601
Telephone: (205) 433-2703
Superintendent: Capt. W. J. Diffley, USN (Ret.)
Hours: Daily 8 A.M. to dusk (ticket office closes one hour earlier); closed Christmas
Cost of admission: Adults (12 years and over) $2.50; under 12 years $1

Description: At the close of World War II the USS *Alabama* (BB-60), a 35,000-ton battleship, led the victorious American fleet into Tokyo Bay. When the battleship was decommissioned in 1947, the governor of Alabama sought to buy the vessel as a memorial. Alabamians everywhere contributed to a million-dollar campaign to bring the famous ship the 5,600 miles from Seattle to Mobile, build a 75-acre park, and prepare the ship for public showing. Since that time the fleet-type submarine USS *Drum* has been added to the park, as have numerous fighting planes of World War II.

Located in Battleship Parkway, Mobile, Ala., the famous USS *Alabama* now lies permanently enshrined. Brought to its resting place through citizens' contributions, this gallant ship was engaged in every battle of the Pacific during World War II without ever receiving a direct hit from an enemy gun of any consequence.

The USS *Alabama* from the air.

CEC SEABEE MUSEUM

Commodore B. W. Fink, Jr., Bldg. 99, Code 2232
Naval Construction Battalion Center, Port
Hueneme, CA 93043
Telephone: (805) 982-5163
Curator: Lt. Comdr. Y. H. Ketels, CEC, USN (Ret.)
Hours: Monday through Friday 8 A.M. to 4:30
P.M.; Saturday 9 A.M. to 4:30 P.M.; Sunday 12:30
P.M. to 4:30 P.M.; closed holidays
Cost of admission: Free to the public

Description: The museum was established in 1947 as a lasting monument to the history and fighting spirit of the Seabees and Naval Civil Engineer Corps. It contains weapons, swords, unusual hunting and farming implements, personal memorabilia, and many other items relating to the customs and culture of the various countries and islands where Seabees have and are still serving. In addition to the souvenirs, the museum features dioramas depicting some of the Seabees' larger construction feats.

Entrance to CEC Seabee Museum.

Admiral Ben Moreell, founder of the U.S. Navy Seabees.

World War II and Korean foes.

The birth of the U.S. Naval Civil Engineer Corps, 1867.

American servicemen from World War II.

SAN FRANCISCO NAVY AND MARINE CORPS MUSEUM

Bldg. 1, Treasure Island, San Francisco, CA 94130
Telephone: (415) 765-6059 or 765-6182
Curator: Stephen M. Harding
Hours: Daily 10:30 A.M. to 3:30 P.M.; closed
Christmas and New Year's Day
Cost of admission: Free to the public
Description: The Navy and Marine Corps Museum is the largest combined services museum in the U.S. It features the history of the Navy and Marine Corps in the Pacific since 1813. Its collection includes armored vehicles, aircraft, weapons of all types and periods, uniforms of the Navy and Marines (as well as Japanese), paintings, prints, documents, decorations, flags, ship and aircraft models, military miniatures, and more. This museum also has the largest collection of artifacts from the Golden Gate International Exposition (held on the island 1939–40) in the U.S., an extensive research library, and a large photo archive.

Exhibits feature life at sea in all its aspects.

SUBMARINE FORCE LIBRARY AND MUSEUM

P.O. Box 16, Naval Submarine Base, Groton, CT 06340
Telephone: (203) 449-3174
Curator: Gary R. Morrison, MMCS(SS), USN
Hours: Monday through Saturday 10 A.M. to 4 P.M.; Sunday and holidays 11 A.M. to 4 P.M.
Cost of admission: Free to those having normal access to the base.

Description: Visiting by the public is not allowed, except on those days with "open-house" hours.

This official U.S. Navy Library and Museum has a great deal of material relating to U.S. Navy submarines in World War II. Its collection also covers the history and development of navy submarines of many nations. The library contains over 8,000 books relating to submarines, flags and pennants carried by famous submarines, a collection of submarine paintings, memorabilia of well-known submariners, many submarine models, including a set of models of U.S. submarines all built to the same scale, from the 54-foot *Holland* (SS-1) to the 448-foot *Triton* (SSN 586). A valuable part of the museum's collection is a file of some 50,000 photographs dealing with submarines and related subjects.

Outdoor exhibits at the Submarine Force Library and Museum.

Model of fleet type submarine of World War II.

U.S. COAST GUARD MUSEUM

New London, CT 06320

Telephone: (203) 443-8463, Ext. 211

Curator: P. H. Johnson

Cost of admission: Free to the public

Description: The museum features Coast Guard memorabilia and artifacts from its founding, through numerous wars, to the present. It tells of the early life-saving service and lighthouse service, and presents an array of models, paintings, equipment, photos, and historic uniforms.

Many nautical paintings are on display at the U.S. Coast Guard Museum.

A liquor-laden British steamer waits off the coast of New Jersey, c. 1930. During Prohibition the Coast Guard was busy enforcing the antismuggling laws.

A sailor on the verge of shooting a line to a disabled fishing vessel.

The Coast Guard comes to the rescue.

TRUXTUN-DECATUR NAVAL MUSEUM

1610 H Street NW, Washington, DC 20006
Telephone: (202) 842-0050
Director: Edmund Curtin
Hours: Daily 10 A.M. to 4 P.M.; closed holidays
Cost of admission: Free to the public
Description: Over half a century ago, a fore-
sighted naval officer, Commdr. Dudley Knox,
wrote an article entitled "Our Vanishing History
and Traditions." In it he detailed "glaring defi-
ciencies" in collecting and preserving the navy's
written records, which had resulted in the wide
"dispersion and deplorable inaccessibility of the
. . . sources of naval history and tradition."
Knox's article led to the formation of the Naval
Historical Foundation in 1926, and, later, the
establishment of its museum. Here is gathered
the largest collection of personal naval papers in
the United States. The museum acts as a repository of naval artifacts and memorabilia. It helps
preserve the heritage of the U.S. Navy, Marine
Corps, Coast Guard, and Merchant Marine.

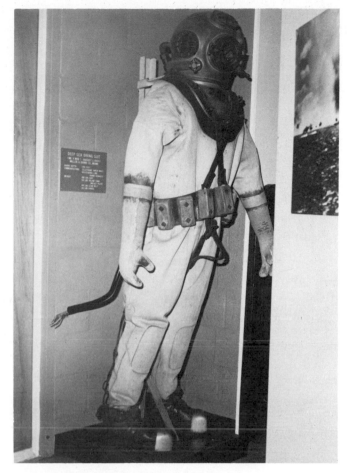

Heavy-duty deep-sea diving outfit on display at Truxtun-
Decatur Naval Museum.

Seaplane models hang from overhead.

U.S. MARINE CORPS MUSEUM, MARINE CORPS HISTORICAL CENTER

Bldg. 58, Washington Navy Yard, Washington, DC 20374

Telephone: (202) 433-3267

Director: F. B. Nihart; Chief Curator: J. B. Hillard

Hours: Monday through Saturday 10 A.M. to 4 P.M.; Sunday and holidays noon to 5 P.M.; summer evening hours 6 P.M. to 8 P.M.

Cost of admission: Free to the public

Description: Museum illustrates, through use of uniforms, weapons, and other military equipage, graphics, art, and documents, a review of the Marine Corps' role in American history. In addition, changing displays of Marine Corps art and topical exhibits of martial artifacts are presented in a separate gallery. A number of additional study collections are located in the museum's ordnance and technology storage and exhibit facility at Quantico, Va.

Building 58, Washington Navy Yard, houses the Marine Corps Historical Center and Museum.

Battleship model.

236

The first case in the Marine Corps Museum's "Time Tunnel" depicts Continental Marines in the Revolution.

Medal display at the Marine Corps Museum.

Marine mementos from the Civil War.

U.S. NAVY MEMORIAL MUSEUM

Bldg. 76, Washington Navy Yard, Washington, DC 20374

Telephone: (202) 433-2651

Associate Director: Oscar P. Fitzgerald

Hours: Monday through Friday 9 A.M. to 4 P.M.; weekends 10 A.M. to 5 P.M.; closed Thanksgiving, Christmas, and New Year's Day

Cost of admission: Free to the public

Description: Started in 1963, this museum now houses over 30,000 feet of indoor exhibits pertaining to all facets of naval history. Large and small weapons, uniforms, artifacts, miniatures, original art, decorations, and nautical charts, plus other historic materials, are on display. Push-button exhibits, with listening devices, are set in light boxes to add sound and motion to many of the displays. The museum is surrounded by a park and the waterfront. In the park are captured Japanese and German 2-man submarines from World War II, large naval guns, and oceanographic submersibles.

Entrance to United States Naval Aviation Museum.

Japanese 2-man submarine, c. 1940.

Ship guns of all caliber.

Space exhibit.

NAVAL AVIATION MUSEUM

Naval Air Station, Pensacola, FL 32508
Telephone: (904) 452-3604
Director: Grover Walker
Hours: Daily 9 A.M. to 5 P.M.; closed Thanksgiving,
Christmas, and New Year's Day
Cost of admission: Free to the public
Description: The Naval Aviation Museum is a shore activity of the U.S. Navy in an active-operating status under the command of the Chief of Naval Air Training. The museum's mission is to select, collect, preserve, and display appropriate memorabilia representative of the development, growth, and heritage of U.S. naval aviation. This museum supplements other national and Department of the Navy museums by projecting the history and traditions of naval aviation to the flight students and others on duty or visiting in the Pensacola naval complex.

Entrance to the U.S. Navy Memorial Museum.

Inside the museum the story of naval aviation is presented in chronological order by use of pictures, charts, diagrams, text, artifacts, personal memorabilia, models, and 25 full-size aircraft. Historical movies on naval aviation are shown in the museum theater daily during the summer months and on weekends and holidays year round at no charge.

Contrasting exhibits of early aviation and space flight.

Navy planes of all vintages.

NAVY SUPPLY CORPS MUSEUM

Navy Supply Corps School, Athens, GA 30606
Telephone: (404) 549-3605
Curator: Capt. Richard P. Pawson, SC, USN (Ret.)
Hours: Monday through Saturday 9 A.M. to 5 P.M.;
Sunday 10 A.M. to 4 P.M.; closed holidays
Cost of admission: Free to the public
Description: On display are memorabilia from the Navy Supply Corps during different periods of American history, including old books, uniforms, artifacts, and historic orders.

Front entrance to Navy Supply Corps Museum.

Picnic grounds.

Displays of naval uniforms.

CONFEDERATE NAVAL MUSEUM

201 4th St. (P.O. Box 1022), Columbus, GA 31902
Telephone: (404) 327-9798
Curator: Robert Holcombe
Hours: Tuesday through Saturday 10 A.M. to 5 P.M.; Sunday 2 P.M. to 5 P.M.; closed Thanksgiving and Christmas
Cost of admission: Free to the public
Description: The museum features the salvaged hulls of Confederate gunboats Jackson ("Muscogee") and Chattahoochee, plus related artifacts, and exhibits, models, and dioramas relating to the Confederate States Navy.

Stern section of the CSS Jackson at Confederate Naval Museum.

A "David" model submarine after the Civil War in Charleston, S.C.

USS *ARIZONA* MEMORIAL

Pearl Harbor, HI 96860
Hours: Tuesday through Sunday; closed national holidays. A Navy-operated boat shuttles visitors to the memorial every half hour from 9 A.M. to 11:30 A.M. and 1 P.M. to 3:30 P.M.
Cost of admission: Free to the public

Description: The memorial was dedicated on Memorial Day 1962 honoring all the U.S. servicemen who lost their lives at Pearl Harbor on December 7, 1941. The Shrine Room wall of the memorial, built over the rusting hull of the battleship *Arizona,* contains the names of 1,177 Navy and Marine Corps men killed when it sank, minutes after being hit. The bodies of more than 1,000 of these men remain entombed.

View of the exterior of the memorial commemorating the sinking of the USS *Arizona* at Pearl Harbor, December 7, 1941.

The Shrine Room wall with the 1,177 names of those killed aboard the USS *Arizona.*

PACIFIC SUBMARINE MUSEUM

Naval Submarine Base, Pearl Harbor, HI 96860
Telephone: (808) 471-0632
Curator: Ray W. de Yarmin
Hours: Daily 9:30 A.M. to 5 P.M.
Cost of admission: Free to the public

Description: The museum exhibits the actual equipment of submarines: the conning tower from USS *Parche* (SS-384) of World War II fame (her skipper, Comdr. "Red" Ramage, was the first live submariner to be awarded the Medal of Honor); an operational periscope; a McCann rescue bell, as used in rescuing members of USS *Squalus* (SS-192) in 1939; Kaiten, the Japanese 1-man suicide torpedo, 54 feet long; a SUBROC missile; numerous documents, photographs, and personal mementos donated by submarine veterans; and a research library (including war patrol reports from World War II submarine action, photographs, and pamphlets). Also open to the public is the submarine Memorial Park containing an exterior display of various types of torpedos and several submarine models.

Superstructure from the USS *Parche* located in the Submarine Memorial Park near the Pacific Submarine Museum.

Kaiten, 1-man Japanese suicide torpedo, 54 feet long. Powered by oxygen with a cruising speed of 40 knots (for the duration of an hour), it carried 3,000 pounds of explosives.

Interior of the museum.

MUSEUM OF SCIENCE AND INDUSTRY

57th St. and Lake Shore Dr., Chicago, IL 60637
Telephone: (312) 684-1414
President and Director: Dr. Victor J. Danilov
Hours: Monday through Friday 9:30 A.M. to 4
P.M.; weekends, holidays and Memorial Day through
Labor Day 9:30 A.M. to 5:30 P.M.
Cost of admission: Free to the public

Description: One of this museum's prized possessions is best described in the words of a World War II combat reporter: "Submarine history was being inscribed in blood and thunder. The unusual became the ordinary. Capt. Daniel V. Gallery, USN, set out to capture a complete, ready-to-go submarine. He accomplished the task by taking captive the German U-505. It was indeed a prize ready for immediate occupancy. There was food in the refrigerators, torpedos in the tubes, and secret code books in the captain's safe. Today, that same submarine can be seen on public display at the Museum of Science and Industry, Chicago." There are numerous other attractions, too many to name, but the U-505 would make any visit a worthwhile affair.

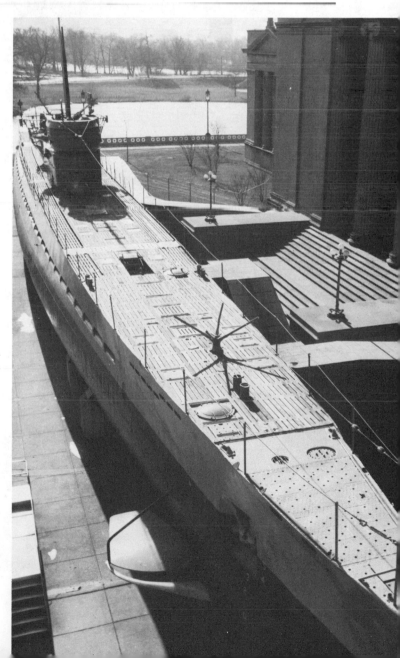

The captured German submarine U-505.

Captain Daniel V. Gallery, Commander of USS *Guadalcanal*, CVE-60, on conning tower of the captured U-505 prior to its being taken in tow.

The U-505 alongside the USS *Guadalcanal*.

U.S. NAVAL ACADEMY MUSEUM

Annapolis, MD 21402
Telephone: (301) 267-2108
Director: Dr. William W. Jefferies
Hours: Tuesday through Saturday 9 A.M. to 4:50
P.M.; Sunday 11 A.M. to 4:50 P.M.; closed
Thanksgiving, Christmas, and New Year's Day
Cost of admission: Free to the public
Description: Utilizing 3-dimensional and graphic materials, the museum demonstrates the navy's role, in war and in peace, in defending and preserving the ideals of our country and mankind. The exhibitions and related research are reminders of our naval heritage—a long record of loyalty, integrity, and service to the nation. There are on display ship models, naval battle prints, naval paintings, uniforms, crystal, silver, firearms, medals, manuscripts, photographs, ships' instruments and gear, and a wide variety of personal memorabilia.

HMS *Duke*, one of the models in the famous Henry Huddleston Rogers Collection at the U.S. Naval Academy Museum.

NAVAL AIR TEST AND EVALUATION MUSEUM

P.O. Box 407, Naval Air Station, Patuxent River,
MD 20670
Telephone: (301) 863-7418
Administrator: K. N. Delhagen
Hours: Tuesday through Saturday noon to 6 P.M.;
Sunday and holidays noon to 5 P.M.
Cost of admission: Free to the public
Description: This museum is conveniently located in Lexington Park just off Rt. 235 at the Patuxent River, Md., Naval Air Station. It houses aircraft systems, and displays related to the test and evaluation of Naval aircraft. It is educational and informative to all groups. Tours are conducted to explain such aircraft as the A-7A, the 13th *Corsair II* built, which logged both speed and altitude records while being tested at Patuxent River.

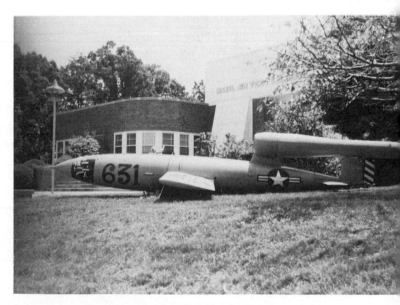

Early rocketry on display in front of Naval Air Test and Evaluation Museum.

Experimental flying machines.

Aircraft carrier model.

USS *CONSTITUTION* MUSEUM

P.O. Box 1812, Charleston, MA 02129
Telephone: (617) 426-1812
Director: Peter V. Sterling
Hours: Daily 9 A.M. to 5 P.M.
Cost of admission: Adults $1.25; children 25¢; senior citizens 50¢
Description: The museum houses artifacts and memorabilia relating to the history of USS *Constitution*, featuring five galleries, many with participatory exhibits that explore the building of *Old Ironsides*, her war years, and life at sea. The art collection includes paintings, prints, and models of the USS *Constitution* and other nautical craft. A photographic mural documents her restoration and preservation. The museum library, open to members and students, includes publications, archival materials, photographs, and microfilm about the construction and history of the USS *Constitution* and the museum. The ship itself, anchored at the Boston Naval Shipyard, is also open to visitors.

Entrance to USS *Constitution* Museum.

The frigate USS *Constitution* in Boston harbor.

PT BOAT MUSEUM AND LIBRARY

Battleship Cove, Fall River, MA 02721

Address inquiries to: National Headquarters, PT Boats, Inc., P.O. Box 109, Memphis, TN 38101

Telephone: Mass.—(617) 678-1100 or Tenn.—(901) 272-9980

Director: J. M. "Boats" Newberry

Hours: Daily 9 A.M. to 5 P.M.; closed Thanksgiving and Christmas

Cost of admission: Adults (15 years and over) $3.60; children $2

Description: PT boats were used as ambush vessels, hunters, marauders, and spy transports; and for rescue, escort duty, ferrying commandos, barge sinking, beachhead invasions, and seeking out and destroying enemy ships regardless of their size. The PT-796 is the last known operable U.S. World War II PT in the world.

PT boat at "flank speed," in excess of 50 knots. This 80-foot Elco PT boat is the same class as John F. Kennedy's PT-109, which was armed with torpedos, 40-mm–37-mm and .50-cal. twin guns, crew of 12 to 18, 3 Packard 1500 h.p. engines, 3 propellers, 3 rudders.

This is the PT used in President John F. Kennedy's inaugural parade with the PT-109 crew members aboard. The PT Museum and Library is located on board the battleship *Massachusetts*.

USS *MASSACHUSETTS* MEMORIAL COMMITTEE, INC.

Battleship Cove, Fall River, MA 02721

Telephone: (617) 678-1100 or 678-1905

Executive Vice-President: Paul S. Vaitses, Jr.

Hours: Daily 9 A.M. to 5 P.M.; closed Thanksgiving and Christmas

Cost of admission: Adults $3.50; children $1.50

Description: Battleship Cove is the only complex with five 20th-century U.S. Navy fighting ships on display. The submarine *Lionfish* arrived in 1972, the destroyer *Joseph P. Kennedy, Jr.,* arrived in 1974, the PT-796 in 1975; followed by the gunboat *Ashville* in 1978. The cove is the largest complex of historic ships in the world. The *Massachusetts* is the largest ship in the complex, being 680 feet long, 108 feet wide, and as tall as a 15-story building. The ship is actually a community in itself, containing all the shops, stores, and other facilities that are to be found in a small city.

USS *Massachusetts* anchored in Battleship Cove.

SALEM MARITIME NATIONAL HISTORIC SITE

U.S. Custom House, Derby St., Salem, MA 01970
Telephone: (617) 744-4323
Curator: John M. Frayler
Hours: Daily 8:30 A.M. to 5 P.M.; closed
Thanksgiving, Christmas, and New Year's Day
Cost of admission: Free to the public

Description: It is impossible to say "war" without thinking of Salem. During the Revolutionary War Salem families, like that of Richard Derby, reaped a profit from privateering. There were over 150 Salem vessels sailing the seas under the striped flag of a privateer. With the signing of a peace treaty, the British closed her ports—and those of her West Indian and other colonies—to American vessels. So Salem shipowners, deprived of their privateer status and without nearby ports, sent vessels to far corners of the world. And the merchants empowered their

Founded in 1626, Salem became the first town in the Massachusetts Bay Colony in 1628, and served for almost 200 years as a hub of trade between America and the world. Pictured here is the Custom House, a central feature of Salem National Historic Site.

captains, some mere lads still in their teens, to act for them as buying and selling agents. The story of Salem, the Revolutionary War, privateering, and postwar merchandising are all beautifully told at this historic site.

USS *NORTH CAROLINA* BATTLESHIP MEMORIAL

P.O. Box 417, Wilmington, NC 28402
Telephone: (919) 762-1829
Curator: Capt. F. S. Conlon, USN (Ret.)
Hours: Daily 8 A.M. to sunset; summer 8 A.M. to 8 P.M.
Cost of admission: Adults $2.50; children (6 to 11 years) $1

Description: The battleship *North Carolina* is located across the Cape Fear River from downtown Wilmington, N.C. It is a famous World War II battleship restored to mint condition; portions of nine decks and levels are open to the public. During the summer months, a sound-and-light spectacular, "The Immortal Showboat," is presented nightly. Over 500 lights and speakers tell the history of the USS *North*

USS *North Carolina*, still standing close to the main channel as if ready to steam off on a mission.

Carolina from her keel-laying to the end of the war. Its silver service was first donated to the armored cruiser USS *North Carolina* by the people of the state in 1908. It is now on display in the Battleship Memorial Museum.

Scout plane.

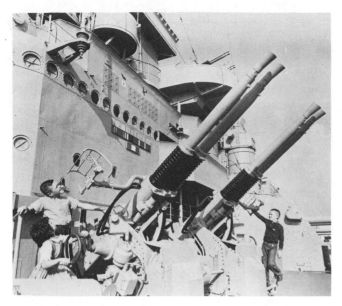

Behind the antiaircraft guns is a scoreboard of enemy kills.

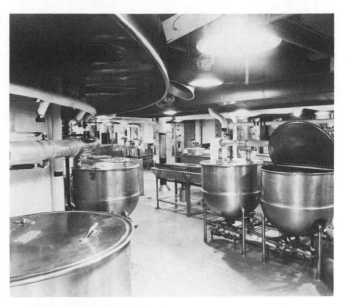

The galley, still kept spotless.

GREAT LAKES HISTORICAL SOCIETY MUSEUM

480 Main St., Vermilion, OH 44089
Telephone: (216) 967-3467
Business Manager: A. N. O'Hara
Hours: Daily 10 A.M. to 5 P.M.
Cost of admission: Adults $1.50; under 16 years 75¢

Description: The museum features paintings pertaining to sailing ships, photographs, builder's half models, and marine relics—all dealing with the Great Lakes. The Commodore Perry Room holds memorabilia of Battle of Lake Erie, War of 1812. There is also a large collection of marine engines, a mural showing 100 years of Great Lakes shipping, and a collection of navigational instruments.

Simulated pilot house of the Great Lakes Historical Society Museum. Overlooking the Vermilion harbor and Lake Erie, the bridge includes a ship's wheel and stand, a binnacle and compass, a gyro compass, a whistle pull, captain's chair, and other equipment from a variety of Great Lakes steamers.

FLAGSHIP NIAGARA

Foot of State St., Erie, PA 16507
Telephone: (814) 871-4596
Curator: William E. Dudenhoefer
Hours: Tuesday through Saturday 10 A.M. to 4:30
P.M.; Sunday noon to 4:30 P.M.; closed major
holidays
Cost of admission: Adults $1; under 12 years and
over 60 years free
Description: Visitors may see and board the restored flagship used by Perry in the Battle of Lake Erie, September 10, 1813. The reconstructed brig *Niagara*, a sturdy little wooden ship, is a symbol of the bravery and enterprise that saved the old Northwest from the British in the War of 1812. This ship is a square-rigged vessel of war with two masts, the foremast standing 92 feet in height and the mainmast 100 feet. On its fighting deck the brig carries 18 carronades and thirty 2-pound guns for close fighting.

ANTIQUE AIRCRAFT DISPLAY

Naval Air Station, Willow Grove, PA 19090
Telephone: (215) 443-1776
Curator: Lt. (j.g.) Deborah A. Becker, USNR
Hours: Daily 24 hours
Cost of admission: Free to the public
Description: The display includes a large collection of captured enemy aircraft from World War II. Planes such as the German AR-196-A-1 coastal patrol plane, the Japanese Nakajima B6N1 torpedo bomber, and the Japanese Kiwanishi NIKI Kyofu Model 11 "Mighty Wind" (Rex 11) floatplane fighter aircraft may be viewed at close quarters.

Experimental search and rescue "Fly Cycle."

PATRIOTS POINT NAVAL AND MARITIME MUSEUM

P.O. Box 986, Mt. Pleasant, SC 29464
Telephone: (803) 884-2727
Executive Director: J. E. Guerry, Jr.; Curator: Clark G. Reynolds
Hours: Daily 9 A.M. to 5 P.M.
Cost of admission: Adults $3.50; children $2.50
Description: From Charleston, just across the Cooper River bridge on Hwy. 17 N., stay to the right at the foot of the bridge, and turn right at the traffic light. The 888-foot 27,100-ton *Yorktown* during World War II carried a crew of 380 officers and 3,088 enlisted men and an air group of 90 planes. In the 1950s she was modified with the addition of an angled deck for jets, which increased her tonnage to 41,000, and then she was converted into an antisubmarine carrier. In this capacity she served in the Vietnam War in the 1960s and recovered the Apollo 8 astronauts, the first men to reach the vicinity of the moon, in 1968. Decommissioned 2 years later, the *Yorktown* was towed from New Jersey to Charleston in 1975. Displays currently aboard the *Yorktown* include many historical artifacts.

Aircraft carrier *Yorktown* at sea.

Ready room aboard the fighting lady.

The *Yorktown* at the harbor's edge in Charleston.

Wardroom aboard the *Yorktown*.

PARRIS ISLAND MUSEUM

P.O. Box 5-036, Parris Island, SC 29905
Telephone: (803) 525-2602
Curator: M. Sgt. Pete Dawson
Hours: Daily 9:15 A.M. to 4:30 P.M.
Cost of admission: Free to the public
Description: The Parris Island Museum is devoted to the portrayal of contemporary Marine Corps training of recruits at Parris Island and the depiction of various Marine Corps contributions during the first 2 centuries of our nation's history. Framed photographs showing early recruit training at Parris Island line the hall leading east from the main floor of the rotunda. In the Weapon Room a selection of weaponry, both old and new, fired at Parris Island by Marines is shown in a unique setting. The Woman Marine Room exhibits uniforms and historical items, photographs, and paintings relating to the growth of the Women Marines since 1918. Photographic displays showing women recruit training at Parris Island are highlighted. Displays of original Marine Corps art and special rotating exhibits occupy 2 additional rooms of the museum.

World War I marine. Marine Corps recruit training at Parris Island was in a full-scale phase as America entered World War I on April 6, 1917. In August of 1917, steel helmets were worn for the first time by the marines fighting in France.

THE ADMIRAL NIMITZ CENTER

328 E. Main St., P.O. Box 777, Fredericksburg, TX 78624
Telephone: (512) 997-4379
Executive Director: Douglass Hubbard
Hours: Daily 8 A.M. to 5 P.M.; closed Christmas and New Year's Day
Cost of admission: Adults $1; children 50¢
Description: The Admiral Nimitz Center is one of the most unusual military museums in the world. It is located in Fredericksburg, Tex., birthplace of Fleet Adm. Chester Nimitz, and is dedicated to the more than 2 million men and women who served under him when he was commander-in-chief of the Pacific during World War II. The center consists of 4 units: The Nimitz Steamboat Hotel contains the museum of the Pacific War, with unique exhibits such as a .45 and flight jacket used by a Doolittle Raider, a Japanese belt of 1,000 stitches, and other artifacts; the Nimitz art gallery of combat art; the Garden of Peace built by the people of Japan; and the History Walk of the Pacific War, lined with relics, among them a Japanese dive bomber, American tanks, Japanese artillery, and other pieces

The Nimitz Steamboat Hotel.

View of the History Walk of the Pacific War.

NORWICH UNIVERSITY MUSEUM

Norwich University, Northfield, VT 05663
Telephone: (802) 485-5011, Ext. 240
Curator: Gary T. Lord
Hours: 2 P.M. to 4 P.M. when university is in session
Cost of admission: Free to the public

Description: The exhibits are designed to interpret the history of Norwich (the oldest private military college in the nation) and the achievements of alumni from 1819 to the present. Collections include personal memorabilia of founder Capt. Alden Partridge and such alumni as Adm. George Dewey and Gen. Grenville Dodge. Special collections include Norwich uniforms, flags, weapons, and military accouterments.

NAVAL AMPHIBIOUS MUSEUM

Naval Amphibious Base, Little Creek, Norfolk, VA 23521

Telephone: (804) 464-8130 or 464-7563

Superintendent: Lt. Comdr. H. A. Wallace/OSC J. M. Stroud

Hours: Weekends and holidays 1 P.M. to 5 P.M.; or by appointment; closed Christmas, New Year's Day, and Easter

Cost of admission: Free to the public

Description: The Naval Amphibious Museum contains a variety of displays on the history and evolution of amphibious warfare. The layout of these displays is chronological, beginning with the earliest known amphibious operation and progressing to post–World War II and Vietnam eras. Outdoor exhibits include amphibious equipment.

Naval Amphibious Museum.

PORTSMOUTH NAVAL SHIPYARD MUSEUM

2 High St., Portsmouth, VA 23705

Telephone: (804) 393-8591

Curator: Mrs. Alice C. Hanes

Hours: Tuesday through Saturday 10 A.M. to 5 P.M.; Sunday and Thanksgiving Day 2 P.M. to 5 P.M.; closed Christmas and New Year's Day

Cost of admission: Free to the public

Description: The museum features ship models, maps, flags, uniforms, medals, navigational instruments, woodworking tools, ordnance, and prints, portraying the history of Portsmouth and the Norfolk Shipyard. The museum is located on the waterfront of the Elizabeth River at the foot of High St.

Front entrance to Portsmouth Naval Shipyard Museum.

NAVAL MUSEUM OF UNDERSEA WARFARE

Naval Undersea Warfare Engineering Station, Keyport, WA 98345
Telephone: (206) 396-2340 or 396-2345
Director: Commanding Officer, Naval Undersea Warfare Station
Hours: By appointment
Cost of admission: Free to the public
Description: Currently on display are 14 torpedos, from the 1889 Howell torpedo to the present Mark 48 Mod 1. Other exhibited items include gyros, gear boxes, control mechanisms, batteries, microcircuitry, a transducer/transmitter/receiver acoustic system, and a warhead; as well as record books and photographs.

Entrance to the Naval Museum of Undersea Warfare.

Torpedo MK 27 MOD 4, in operation from 1950 to 1962.

Cutaway view of Torpedo MK 44 MOD 1.

Part III

AIR MUSEUMS

ALABAMA SPACE AND ROCKET CENTER

Tranquility Base, Huntsville, AL 35807
Telephone: (205) 837-3400
Director: Edward O. Buckbee
Hours: Daily, September through May 9 A.M. to 5 P.M.; June through August 8 A.M. to 6 P.M.; closed Christmas
Cost of admission: Nominal fee charged, with varying rates for entire family, senior citizens, students, etc.

Description: The world's largest space museum, the Alabama Space and Rocket Center, features over $30 million worth of space hardware, including the historic *Saturn V* moon rocket and *Apollo 16* command module. America's first lady in space, Monkeynaut Baker, is in residence. Over 50 hand-maneuvered space-age instruments let you actively explore the unknown worlds around us. A guided tour of nearby Marshall Space Flight Center, NASA's largest field installation, is offered several times daily so visitors can see actual space-related work taking place.

Alabama Space and Rocket Center.

Simulated flight to the moon.

Monkeynaut Baker, one of the first monkeys to complete a successful space flight.

PIMA AIR MUSEUM

6400 S. Wilmot Rd., P. O. Box 17298, Tucson, AZ 85731

Telephone: (602) 889-0462 or 889-0646

Director: George C. Shott, Jr.; Curator: Robert A. Johnson

Hours: Daily, winter 9 A.M. to 5 P.M.; summer 8 A.M. to 6 P.M.; admittance only up to 45 minutes before closing

Cost of admission: Adults $2; 12 to 17 years 75¢

Description: Take I-10 to Wilmot Rd., exit 269. Turn north on Wilmot. Continue for 2 miles. (Wilmot Rd. is not a through street.) To visit here is to see the largest collection of fighter and bomber aircraft in the west. Aircraft such as the Boeing Superfortress, the Republic Thunderstreak, and the North American Super Saber are among the more than 100 planes on display. In addition, a reconstructed World War II barracks houses displays on aviation history, equipment, uniforms, models, and artifacts of the air.

Boeing Stratoliner.

North American Saberjet.

Consolidated Liberator.

PACIFIC MISSILE TEST CENTER PARK

Point Mugu, CA 93042
Public Affairs Officer: Lt. Comdr. T. D. Stuart
Cost of admission: Free to the public
Description: The test center has a missile park that is located outside Gate 2 on the access road to Point Mugu adjacent to Hwy. 1. The missiles displayed in the park are the Bullpup A and B, Hawk, Lark, Oriole, Sidewinder, Sparrow I, Sparrow III, Regulus I and II, Polaris A1, Harpoon, Phoenix, and Skyflash.

Front entrance to Aerospace Historical Center.

INTERNATIONAL AEROSPACE HALL OF FAME

2001 Pan American Plaza, Balboa Park, San Diego, CA 92101
Telephone: (714) 232-8322 or 232-1388
Executive Director: Col. E. F. Carey, Jr.
Hours: Daily 10 A.M. to 5 P.M.; weekends and holidays 10 A.M. to 4 P.M.
Cost of admission: $1
Description: The Hall of Fame is situated in renowned Balboa Park, a cultural center containing museums of science, history, and art. It is part of the San Diego Aerospace Museum, which houses one of the world's finest collections of historical aircraft. This Hall of Fame was chartered as the instrument to inspire in the youth of today and tomorrow a respect for the qualities and ethics that guided aerospace heroes and to promote public appreciation of the significant role that aviation and space technology have played in the history of man.

A flying replica of the *Spirit of St. Louis.*

Indoor display, Aerospace Hall of Fame.

SAN DIEGO AEROSPACE MUSEUM

2001 Pan American Plaza, Balboa Park, San Diego, CA 92101
Telephone: (714) 234-8291
Executive Director: Col. Owen F. Clarke, USAF (Ret.)
Hours: Vary according to month of year
Cost of admission: Adults $1
Description: Museum exhibits are arranged chronologically, featuring dynamic displays of pre–World War I, World War I itself, the golden age of flying (1920s and 1930s), World War II, and the space age. The courtyard displays larger aircraft and rocketry. Visitors may browse through the library, see films in the theater, and renew acquaintances in the forum. There are artifacts to be seen (civil, military, antique, and historical), including a replica of the *Spirit of St. Louis*. There is also a Hall of Fame with portraits of many outstanding pilots.

U.S. AIR FORCE ACADEMY VISITOR CENTER

USAFA/PAMCV, USAF Academy, CO 80840
Telephone: (303) 472-2555
Curator: Art Gagnon
Hours: Hours vary according to season of year; closed Thanksgiving, Christmas, and New Year's Day
Cost of admission: Free to the public
Description: The visitor center houses exhibits and a theater showing development of USAFA and explaining cadet life. Collections in Arnold Hall in the cadet area contain memorabilia from Gen. Henry "Hap" Arnold, Jacqueline Cochran, President Dwight D. Eisenhower, and Vietnam POWs. Arnold Hall also houses many historical paintings from Air Force collection and a theater that runs films on cadet life and history of USAFA.

Men in formation at the U.S. Air Force Academy.

Famed statue that reads "Man's flight through life is sustained by the power of his knowledge."

Color guard.

BRADLEY AIR MUSEUM

Bradley International Airport, Windsor Locks, CT 06096

Telephone: (203) 623-3305

Director: Philip C. O'Keefe

Cost of admission: Varies according to number of aircraft being returned to display

Description: At 2:56 P.M., October 3, 1979, the Bradley Air Museum was devastated by a tornado. All of the 58 aircraft on display, part of the 4th largest collection in the country, plus engines and other related exhibits were damaged, with nearly half severely marred or completely destroyed. All public facilities were destroyed or damaged beyond repair. However, recovery work goes on. The museum expects to be operating indoor and outdoor exhibit areas on a temporary site until its new complex can be built. Numerous new and replacement aircraft are expected to arrive within the next few months. Examples include XF4U-4 Corsair, B-29A, F-100A, B-47E. Early aircraft such as Bleriot XI and Gee Bee Model A will return to display as soon as repairs are completed.

NATIONAL AIR AND SPACE MUSEUM

6th and Independence Ave. SW, Washington, DC 20560

Telephone: (202) 381-6264

Director: Dr. Noel W. Hinners

Hours: Daily 10 A.M. to 5:30 P.M.; closed Christmas

Cost of admission: Free to the public

Description: The museum's collection encompasses more than 250 historic or technically significant aircraft, 50 spacecraft, 50 missiles and rockets, 450 aircraft engines, 350 propellers, hundreds of scale models, aviation instruments, flight equipment, and unique memorabilia of famous inventors, airmen, astronauts, and events. Only a portion of the entire collection is on display at any one time; a significant number is on loan to other museums throughout the world. The artifacts on display are arranged throughout 23 exhibit galleries arranged by topics from World War I and II to balloons and airships to rocketry and space flight.

Rockets reach for the stars in the National Air and Space Museum's Space Hall. Objects on display include (clockwise, left to right): Scout, Vanguard, and Jupiter-C launch vehicles; the Skylab Orbital Workshop; and the V-1 "Buzz Bomb."

The Wright 1909 Military Flyer was the world's first military airplane. Suspended in the Early Flight gallery, the Flyer "soars over" an exhibit booth depicting the engines and flight hardware of the Wright Company of Dayton, Ohio.

An Albatros D.Va, one of two remaining in the world, sits in front of a re creation of World War I forward airfield's primitive hangar tent. The Albatros, in its various models, was a mainstay of the German Air Force and was flown by von Richthofen for most of his career.

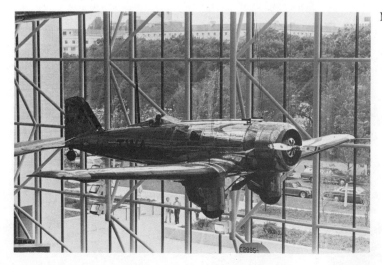

Northrup Alpha.

USAF ARMAMENT MUSEUM

Eglin AFB, FL 32542
Telephone: (904) 882-4062 or 882-4063
Curator: John Sherwin
Hours: Tuesday through Saturday 9 A.M. to 4:15
P.M.; Sunday and Monday 12:30 P.M. to 4:15
P.M.; closed Thanksgiving, Christmas, New Year's
Day, and Easter
Cost of admission: Free to the public
Description: The museum is directly on the right through the east gate (from Valparaiso/Nice-ville). If coming through the west gate (from Fort Walton Beach) proceed through the base on Eglin Pkwy. and take last left turn before leaving the base through east gate. The armament museum is dedicated to collecting, preserving, and displaying historical aircraft weapons and weapon delivery systems. Displays, ranging in time from the early days of the Wright brothers to sophisticated missiles and rockets, will enhance viewer understanding of the equipment and capabilities of the U.S. Air Force.

Airplane park in front of U.S. Air Force Armament Museum.

Hughes GAR-1-D "Falcon" missile shown immediately after firing from a Convair F-102 "Delta Dagger."

Captain E. V. Rickenbacker standing by a Spad plane.

270

SST AIR EXHIBIT

Rt. 1, #10, Aeronautical Dr., Kissimmee, FL 32741
Telephone: (305) 846-2625
Director: J. E. Jacks
Hours: Daily 9 A.M. to 6 P.M.; closed Christmas
Cost of admission: Adults $2.50; children $1
Description: The exhibit features a Boeing SST mockup 288 feet long, 5 stories high; a mural (panorama of flight) 265 feet long; over 600 models; an SST engine built by Pratt and Whitney, plus many other engines; a Mooney Mite; Nate Saint's Taylor E2 (1935); a Formula One Lovin' Love; a Red Baron replica; a B-25, an Albatross/Beech 18; a Supersonic Sea Dart; a Matador missile, a Snark missile and Mercury capsule.

CHANUTE TECHNICAL TRAINING DISPLAY CENTER

Public Affairs Office, Stop 7, Chanute AFB, IL 61868
Telephone: (217) 495-3324
Hours: Weekends 9 A.M. to 5 P.M.
Cost of admission: Free to the public
Description: To take care of today's aircraft and missile weapons—to ready them for launching, to check the intricate guidance systems, the complicated electrical and hydraulic systems, or the unbelievably powerful jet and missile propulsion systems—the skills of thousands of highly trained men and women are required. Chanute works around the clock to provide a key part of this training. Each of Chanute's 4 technical training groups is represented in the display center. The display center even offers a taste of the past. A pictorial history of Chanute, old World War I planes, and an old bomber trainer give visitors an idea of what Chanute Field was once like.

Missile display in front of Chanute Technical Training Display Center.

Jet engine maintenance displays.

Materials and equipment used in jet aircraft.

KALAMAZOO AVIATION HISTORY MUSEUM

2101 E. Milham, Kalamazoo, MI 49002
Telephone: (616) 382-6555
Curator: Suzanne D. Parish
Hours: Wednesday 2 P.M. to 8 P.M.; Thursday 2 P.M. to 5 P.M.; Sunday 2 P.M. to 6 P.M.; closed holidays
Cost of admission: Adults $3; children $1
Description: To reach the museum, travel on I-94 to exit 78 (Portage Rd. exit). Take the south ramp off I-94 onto Portage Rd., then proceed past the entrance of the Municipal Airport to Milham Rd. Turn east (left) on Milham and drive ¼ mile to parking area for museum. This aviation museum is dedicated to educating the public about the contribution of air power to Allied successes in World War II and to preserving aviation heritage for present and future generations. Numerous fighter aircraft are on exhibit, such as the F8F-1 Bearcat, the F6F-5 Hellcat, the FM-2 Wildcat, the N2S-5 Stearman, and many others.

Boeing P-26 in a dive.

North American F-51s of the Air National Guard lined up on the runway during an Air National Guard Gunnery Exercise.

STRATEGIC AIR COMMAND MUSEUM

2510 Clay St., Bellevue, NB 68005

Telephone: (402) 292-2001

Director: Carl A. Janssen

Hours: Daily 8 A.M. to 5 P.M.; closed Christmas, New Year's Day, and Easter

Cost of admission: Adults $2; children $1

Description: The Strategic Air Command Museum is easily reached by travelers coming from the east or west on I-80, and from the north or south on I-29. This museum portrays those first breathtaking seconds at Kitty Hawk, the crushing blow of the massive B-17 attacks on Nazi Germany, and the drama of man's ascent into space. Its displays offer a fascinating look at the trials and triumphs of the U.S. Air Force and the Strategic Air Command. A visitor learns about such giants of the sky as Billy Mitchell, Curtis LeMay, and Jimmy Doolittle. Of special interest is the 5-screen reenactment of an SAC red alert. Outside, you'll find an impressive collection of historic fighters, bombers, missiles, cargo planes, trainers, and rescue and experimental aircraft—all awaiting inspection.

A parking lot for yesteryear's bombers at the Strategic Air Command Museum.

Helicopters, gliders, and jets are all on display.

A one-type bomber.

NATIONAL ATOMIC MUSEUM

Bldg. 20358, S. Wyoming Blvd., Kirtland Air Force Base, NM 87115
Telephone: (505) 844-8443
Director: Carrol V. Canfield; Curator: Lynnie Grace
Hours: Daily 9 A.M. to 5 P.M.; closed Thanksgiving,
Christmas, New Year's Day, and Easter
Cost of admission: Free to the public
Description: The museum features displays on programs under research by the Department of Energy, such as solar energy, geothermal energy, and nuclear energy, and an atomic weapons exhibit, as well as models of the atomic bombs dropped on Japan during World War II.

"Little Boy," a model of the bomb that devastated Hiroshima on August 6, 1945.

"Fat Man," a model of the Nagasaki bomb.

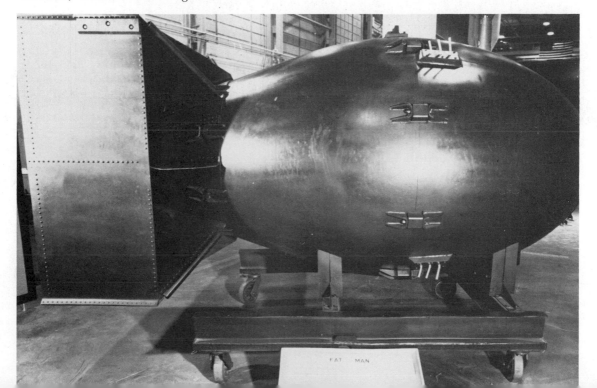

WHITE SANDS MISSILE RANGE MISSILE PARK

STEWS-PA, White Sands Missile Range, NM 88002
Telephone: (505) 678-1134 or 678-1135
Director: James Eckles
Hours: Monday through Friday 7:45 A.M. to 4 P.M.; weekends and holidays 1 P.M. to 5 P.M.
Cost of admission: Free to U.S. citizens—not open to foreign nationals
Description: The missile park is an outdoor display of missile and rocket airframes, including a V-2, and past and current rockets and missiles from the Air Force, Army, and Navy.

Missile Park at White Sands Missile Range.

THE GLENN H. CURTISS MUSEUM

Lake and Main sts., Hammondsport, NY 14840
Telephone: (607) 569-2160
Director: Merrill Stickler
Hours: Monday through Saturday 9 A.M. to 5 P.M.
Cost of admission: Adults $2; students $1; children 50¢
Description: The Glenn Hammond Curtiss Museum's primary purpose is education. Although the museum contains a blend of aviation history and memorabilia of what has been termed the "age of homespun," it seeks to give the public a better idea of the enormous contributions to American aviation made by Glenn Curtiss, one of the great American aviation pioneers. A World War I Curtiss "Jenny" training plane, almost every variation of Curtiss OX-5 motor, and a glass-plate slide collection of Lt. Harry Benner, USN, are a few of the items to be seen in this museum; as is Rear Adm. Lansing J. Callan's collection of photographs on early aviation.

Entrance to the Glenn H. Curtiss Museum.

276

Replica of Curtiss 1908 "June Bug."

Curtiss JN4-D.

1910 Hanriot pioneer period aircraft.

OLD RHINEBECK AERODROME

P.O. Box 89, Stone Church Rd., Rhinebeck, NY 12572

Telephone: (914) 758-8610

Director: Cole Palen

Hours: Daily 10 A.M. to 5 P.M.; weekend air show 2:30 P.M.

Cost of admission: Adults $1.50; children $1; air show, adults $4; children $2

Description: This is a living museum of old combat aircraft from the early 1900s to 1937, including pioneer, World War I, and Lindbergh era airplanes. During weekend air shows many of these historically significant aircraft are flown in mock combat. There are two museum buildings full of old airplanes, engines, cars, and related vehicles of the period.

Flight line at Old Rhinebeck Aerodrome before show.

World War I Fokker triplane.

278

WRIGHT BROTHERS NATIONAL MEMORIAL

Address inquiries to: Cape Hatteras National Seashore Group, Rt. 1, Box 675, Manteo, NC 27954

Telephone: (919) 441-7430

Hours: Daily 9 A.M. to 5 P.M.

The first flight by man with a motor-driven, heavier-than-air machine, at Kitty Hawk, N.C., December 17, 1903.

Cost of admission: Free to the public

Description: The visitor center/museum houses exhibits and articles relating to the Wright brothers' early activities; there is also a life-size reproduction of the 1902 glider and 1903 Kitty Hawk Flyer. This is a must stop for any student with a serious interest in the development of military aviation.

CRAWFORD AUTO-AVIATION MUSEUM

10825 East Blvd., Cleveland, OH 11420

Telephone: (216) 721-5722

Curator: Kenneth Gooding

Hours: Tuesday through Saturday 10 A.M. to 5 P.M.; Sunday noon to 6 P.M.

Cost of admission: Adults $2; students $1; Golden Age $1

Description: The museum is conveniently located in the heart of University Circle, Cleveland. Coming from the west on the Ohio turnpike, exit at I-71 and proceed north to I-90. Take I-90 east on Liberty Blvd. and proceed to 105th. Coming from the east on the Ohio turnpike, exit at Streetsboro and proceed north on I-480 to I-271. From I-271 proceed to I-90 west and exit

Roscoe Turner's speed plane of the 1930s.

at Liberty Blvd. Take Liberty to East Blvd. at E. 105th. You will find an impressive display of military bicycles, motorcycles, and planes from the 1890s to the present, including a 1910 Curtiss "Bumble Bee" flown by Albert Engel; a 1917 Curtiss "Flying Boat"; and a Mustang P-51 fighter plane flown in the Thompson Trophy Race of 1946; plus many more.

Formation of Douglas A-24 airplanes.

U.S. AIR FORCE MUSEUM

Wright-Patterson AFB, Dayton, OH 45433
Telephone: (513) 255-3284
Curator: Royal D. Frey
Hours: Monday through Friday 9 A.M. to 5 P.M.;
weekends and holidays 10 A.M. to 6 P.M.
Cost of admission: Free to the public
Description: There are 15,103 items on display. All are memorabilia portraying the history of flight in military aviation. Today this institution is internationally recognized as the world's oldest and largest military museum. It originated in 1923 with an informal exhibition of World War I planes and equipment. In the late 1950s, the museum transformed from a huge open warehouse display to a uniquely designed interior maze floor plan that directs visitors along a controlled walkway, unfolding the story of military aviation in chronological sequence. In addition to a full-scale exact reproduction of the Wright Brothers 1909 Military Flyer, there are a number of items associated with the two famous brothers. Important planes of World War I, such as the Jenny and the Spad, are exhibited.

The Air Force Museum as seen from the air.

World War I mechanic spinning the prop.

World War II observation balloon.

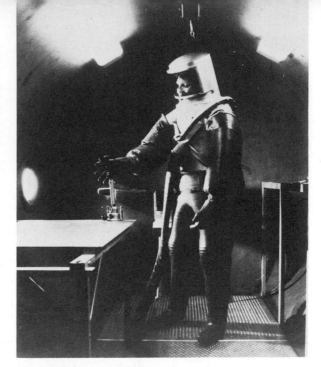

The Mark I U.S. Air Force model "Extra Vehicular and Lunar Surface Suit."

NEIL ARMSTRONG AIR & SPACE MUSEUM

P.O. Box 1978, Wapak-Fisher Rd., Wapakoneta, OH 45895

Telephone: (419) 738-8811

Curator: John Zwez

Hours: Monday through Saturday 9:30 A.M. to 5 P.M.; Sunday and holidays 11 A.M. to 5 P.M.; closed Thanksgiving, Christmas, and New Year's Day

Cost of admission: Adults $1.50; children (6 to 12 years) 75¢

Description: The first gallery features symbols of Ohio air and space achievements. The era of balloon flight is recalled by a balloon basket and trophies won by Dayton balloonist Warren Rasor. Suspended from the ceiling is the large dirigible air frame from the *Toledo II,* the first manned and powered flying machine to grace New York City skies. A reconstructed Wright Brothers Model G Aero-boat, built in Dayton and flown from the Miami River in 1913, is a unique reminder of the pioneering achieve-

First military airplane, the forerunner of the Army Air Force's fleet of military aircraft. The original version of this Wright Brothers 1909 plane employed skids for landing and takeoff, and had its elevators in front of the wings. In 1910 it was modified to incorporate the wheeled landing gear, and the elevators were moved to the rear.

ments of the Dayton, Ohio, brothers. In several other galleries are presented the 1946 Aeronca 7AC Champion in which Neil Armstrong learned to fly, a Jupiter rocket engine, and the *Gemini VIII* spacecraft.

MUSEUM OF FLIGHT MEDICINE

Brooks AFB, TX 78235
Telephone: (512) 536-2203
Director: John W. Bullard
Hours: Monday through Friday 8 A.M. to 4 P.M.;
closed holidays
Cost of admission: Free to the public
Description: Brooks Air Force Base is just outside of San Antonio, Tex. In this museum there are more than 5,000 items showing the development of flight medicine. Through a collection of restored medical memorabilia, artifacts, and displays, an interesting story unfolds. This story describes how man, capable of producing planes engineered to fly at 50,000 feet, cruise at transonic speeds, and climb several miles a minute, must himself have physical aids. To explain problems and solutions, displays take the onlooker through a progression of steps. A large technical and nontechnical library is available for use by serious researchers.

Museum of Flight Medicine building, hangar 9.

Resuscitator exhibit.

Couch used for animal flight into space.

282

The story of medicine as it relates to man in flight.

NASA LYNDON B. JOHNSON SPACE CENTER

Houston, TX 77058

Telephone: (713) 483-4321

Hours: Daily 9 A.M. to 4 P.M.; closed Christmas

Cost of admission: Free to the public

Description: The Johnson Space Center (JSC) is located in the heart of the Clear Lake Area, 4 miles east of I-45 on NASA Road One. The first stop on a visit to JSC is the visitor center, Bldg. 2. The visitor center holds a collection of actual space hardware, as well as educational exhibits about America's space program. NASA films are also shown throughout the day in the center's 800-seat auditorium. On display is the tiny Mercury capsule that carried Astronaut Gordon Cooper on his historic flight, orbiting the earth 22 times before splashing down in the Pacific Ocean. Not far away is the spaceship *America,* the spacecraft that carried the Apollo 17 astronauts—the last scheduled Apollo flight—to the moon. Samples of rocks brought back from the moon are also on display.

A model of the space shuttle.

America: a portrait from space.

The *Apollo 17* Command Module *America*, used in the last scheduled Apollo moon flight.

HISTORY AND TRADITION MUSEUM

Air Force Military Training Center, Lackland AFB, TX 78236

Telephone: (512) 671-3055 or 671-3444

Curator: Gloria M. Livingston

Hours: Monday through Friday 7:30 A.M. to 4 P.M.; weekends 9 A.M. to 6 P.M.; closed Thanksgiving, Christmas, and New Year's Day

Cost of admission: Free to the public

Description: The museum is situated on Orville Wright Dr., Lackland AFB, west of the main entrance. I-410 S., U.S. Hwy. 90 west, and S.W. Military Drive (Loop 13) all lead to Lackland Air Force Base. The museum is a collection of rare aeronautical equipment. These exhibits of aircraft, engines, instruments, and air weapons span the years of aviation development from its origin to the aerospace age. Over 50 aircraft and missiles are statically displayed throughout the base.

The F-80, America's first jet aircraft to be manufactured in large quantities. Although produced too late for World War II, the "Shooting Star" was used extensively during the Korean War.

Liberty engine display at the History and Tradition Museum. A 12-cylinder Vee engine, it was the first production model American-designed and -built military aircraft engine. It was the standard engine from 1918 to 1936, and was used to drive British and Russian tanks in World War II (1941–42).

The F-105 "Thunderchief." The F-105D, known as the "Thud," was used extensively in Southeast Asia as a fighter-bomber.

A Mace, surface-to-surface, tactical missile. Developed in 1954, it entered production in 1958.

NASA VISITOR CENTER

Langley Research Center, Mail Stop 480, Hampton, VA 23665

Telephone: (804) 827-2855 or 827-3358

Director: George E. Hicks

Hours: Monday through Saturday 8:30 A.M. to 4:30 P.M.; Sunday noon to 4:30 P.M.; closed Christmas and New Year's Day

Cost of admission: Free to the public

Description: The NASA Visitor Center serves the

The NASA Langley Visitor Center.

public as an interpretive educational facility fostering an understanding of NASA's research and experimentation as well as the technological utilization of the data gained. This is accomplished through a network of displays, NASA publications, and educational programs. Exhibit areas are: Aeronautical Research, Space Program, Technology Utilization, and Solar Energy (Technology Utilization House). The NASA Visitor Center also provides special interest films, publications on NASA programs, no-cost telelectures (slide lectures via telephonic hookup), and Outreach (on-site) programs.

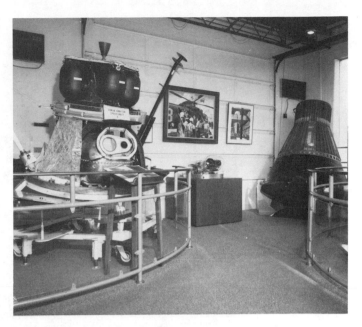

The Lunar Orbiter Spacecraft and camera equipment are on display, along with the Mercury "Joe" capsule.

The *Apollo 12* command module, the *Yankee Clipper*. Launched on November 14, 1969, it set down 4 days later on the moon's surface with astronauts Charles Conrad, Jr., and Alan Bean aboard.

The suit worn by Astronaut David R. Scott on the *Apollo 15* lunar mission.

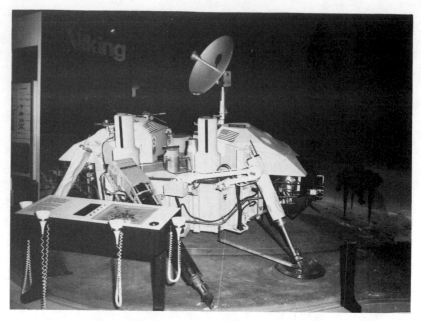

A model of the Viking Lander, one of two that landed on Mars in 1976 equipped with 10 scientific instruments for gathering data.

MARINE CORPS AVIATION MUSEUM

Marine Corps Development and Education Command, Quantico, VA 22134

Telephone: (703) 640-2606

Director: Col. Tom D'Andrea

Hours: Daily 10 A.M. to 4 P.M.; closed Christmas and Easter

Cost of admission: Free to the public

Description: The aviation museum consists of two separate museums, one devoted to the World War II period and one to the "Early Years" (1912–40). In these museums are displayed aircraft, weapons, uniforms, dioramas, and artifacts that were used by Marines, their allies, and their enemies. Among aircraft exhibited are a Japanese Zero, a U.S. Corsair, a Gulf Hawk, and a DH4. Surrounding the museums, which are housed in authentic 1920 hangars, are aircraft and tanks. To the rear of the World War II Museum is a small park commemorating Marine Medal of Honor recipients.

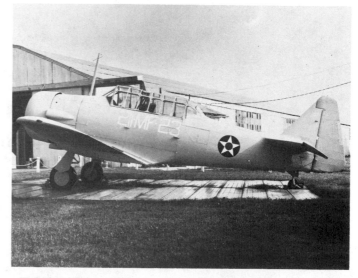

T-6 SNJ "Texan," Marine Corps Aviation Museum.

French "Penguin" ground trainer, 1917.

Squadron insignia, World War II.

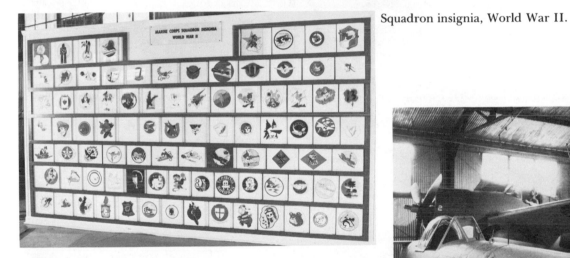

Japanese "Baka" bomb.

Life-size model of an operations tent complex in the Pacific, 1942.

EAA AIR MUSEUM FOUNDATION

11311 W. Forest Home Ave., Franklin, WI 53132
Telephone: (414) 425-4860
Curator: Paul H. Poberezny
*Hours: Monday through Saturday 8:30 A.M. to 5
P.M.; Sunday 11 A.M. to 5 P.M.*
Cost of admission: Adults $2; children 75¢
Description: World's largest privately funded aviation museum, this facility houses a magnificent collection—from the world's smallest aircraft to fine replicas of the Wright Flyer and the *Spirit of St. Louis.* A large sport aviation collection is also on display.

Military and civilian aviation are nicely blended to show the progress of aviation at the EAA Air Museum Foundation.

German fighter planes from World Wars I and II.

WARREN AIR FORCE BASE MILITARY MUSEUM

P.O. Box 9625, Warren AFB, WY 82001
Telephone: (307) 775-2980
Curator: Edward A. Tarbell
Hours: Hours vary
Cost of admission: Free to the public
Description: This is a people-oriented museum with displays of military hardware and artifacts.

There are room displays showing typical quarters and BOQ (bachelor officers' quarters) rooms from the Indian War frontier army. Displays are built around old Fort Russel and Camp Carlin, dating from 1867. An Air Force collection features the 90th Bomb Group, the "Jolly Rogers" of World War II, and a comprehensive aircraft model display which is on loan to the 4th Air Division (SAC). Tours are also conducted through the old post cemetery, which has been active since the first burial in October 1867.

This Flying Boeing B-17 Fortress, with its starboard wing breaking between the engines, is being engulfed in flames that prevented the crew from opening parachutes. The picture was taken from another plane in the formation, on a bomb run over Nis, Yugoslavia, in April 1944.

Part IV

OVERSEAS
MUSEUMS

2ND INFANTRY DIVISION MUSEUM

Bldg. T-8 on Casey Blvd., Camp Casey, Republic of Korea, APO San Francisco, CA 96224
Telephone: Camp Casey (229) 3588
Superintendent: Public Affairs Officer, 2nd Inf. Division
Hours: Wednesday through Friday 8 A.M. to 5 P.M.; Saturday 10 A.M. to 5 P.M.; Sunday 1 P.M. to 5 P.M.
Cost of admission: Free to the public

Description: The 2nd Infantry Division Museum illustrates the pride the men of this unit have in their illustrious past. Memorabilia show their biography from the Indian Wars of the mid-1800s to the Korean War. A special Korean War Room indicates the ever-present threat of hostilities occurring again in this area of the world. Among the mementos to be seen are the ornate Liscum Bowl, which weighs 90 pounds, made of silver given to the 9th Infantry Regiment by a prince of China after the Boxer Rebellion; a map board that shows the routes and campaigns of the "Indianhead" Division during World War I, World War II, and the Korean War; and Nazi items of combat captured in Europe.

Larger weapons, such as cannons, howitzers, and tanks, are displayed outside the 2nd Infantry Division Museum building at Camp Casey, Republic of Korea.

The cultural center room offers for viewing the four valuable silver regimental bowls, Korean antiques, contemporary items of "historical value," and a gallery of all past division commanders.

The pre-1920 room houses artifacts from the Indian Wars, the American Civil War, the Boxer Rebellion, the Philippine Insurrection, the Spanish-American War, and World War I.

Nazi memorabilia, including German Veterans Association flag, captured during the last months of World War II.

A poplar tree stump helps visitors recall the brutal killing of two officers by North Korean soldiers in 1976. The display shows, in photographs taken from an observation post, how the officers were overcome by the North Koreans while the United Nations command personnel were attempting to prune the large poplar tree that was obscuring the view of an official observation point.

U.S. ARMED FORCES MUSEUM

Address inquiries to: Historian/Museum Curator, Headquarters, U.S. Army Garrison, Okinawa, APO San Francisco, CA 96331

Hours: Tuesday through Sunday noon to 5 P.M.; closed federal holidays

Cost of admission: Free to the public

Description: This Armed Forces museum, devoted to the battle for Okinawa during World War II, displays American and Japanese equipment from the battlefield including heavy machine guns. A large 1/15,000 terrain map, with automated lights identifying specific turning points in the battle for Okinawa, is keyed to a tape recording (available in 9 languages) narrating the movement of the battle in the final phase. The cultural room illustrates various aspects of postwar Ryukyuan cultural, agricultural, and industrial achievements.

Interior of the Armed Forces Museum on Okinawa.

SAN JUAN NATIONAL HISTORIC SITE

P.O. Box 712, Old San Juan, Puerto Rico 00902

Executive Director: Doel R. Garcia

Hours: Vary according to individual site

Cost of admission: Varies with each site, but generally a small fee

Description: Old San Juan, Puerto Rico, was built in 1521. Most of it still remains a walled city, with fortifications pointed toward the defense of San Juan Bay. As a result there are several old forts, each a military museum within itself. El Morro, greatest of the defenses, is a single unit with 6 levels rising 140 feet above the sea. Fort San Jeronimo, a much smaller bastion, has been restored and converted into a military museum; it is complete with ship models, old charts, documents, uniformed mannequins, weapons, and ancient pieces of artillery.

Aerial view of the fortress of San Felipe del Morro.

296

"OLD IRONSIDES" MUSEUM

Katterbach, West Germany
Address inquiries to: Headquarters 1st Armored
Division, APO NY 09326
Curator: Daniel E. Lemin
Hours: Daily 9 A.M. to 4 P.M.
Cost of admission: Free to the public

Description: The museum features predominantly German and American weapons, uniforms, medals, insignia, documents, photos, and memorabilia from World War II, plus some from World War I. Exhibits illustrate the development of armored fighting forces and the role of the U.S. 1st Armored Division in World War II.

A scout dog and his handler participate in a mock gas attack during maneuvers in Germany.

PICTURE CREDITS

Numerals refer to page numbers. Key letters refer to the position of the picture on the page: t, *top;* c, *center;* b, *bottom;* l, *left;* r, *right. Photographs for which no credits are given are courtesy of the author.*

Aiken Standard, 255r

Alabama Bureau of Publicity and Information, 2t, 2c, 2b, 3, 8t, 8b, 9t

Armed Forces Institute of Pathology, 27

Pat Bauer, 20

N. John Charpentier, 242t

D. Pat Cheatham, 181t

Frederick C. Crawford Auto-Aviation Museum, 279b

Game, Fish, and Parks Department, 171

Steve Grams, 183t, 183b

Rev. Arthur A. Guenther, 16b

Harpers Ferry National Historical Park, 220t, 220bl, 220br

Haycox Photoramic, Inc., 191tl, 200b

Paul Kivett, Landmarks Commission, Kansas City, Mo., 105

Museum of Science and Industry, Chicago, 245b

NASA, 286b, 287t, 287b, 288tl, 288tr

Nebraska Game and Parks Commission, 112b, 113tl, 113tr

Nebraska State Historical Society, 113b

New York State Office of Parks and Recreation, 124

Oregon Department of Transportation, 158t, 158b

Pacific Submarine Museum, 244t, 244b, 245t

John H. Sheally II, 200t

Smithsonian Institution, 268t, 268b, 269t, 269b

State Historical Society of Wisconsin, 222t

Larry Syler, 181b

U.S. Air Force, 270t, 270c, 270b, 272b, 273t, 273b, 279t, 280t, 281cr, 291

U.S. Army, x, 7t, 7b, 16t, 22t, 24b, 31t, 31c, 31b, 48, 49t, 49b, 50, 54t, 54b, 55t, 62b, 63t, 63b, 64t, 64b, 65t, 65c, 68t, 69b, 70t, 117b, 118t, 118c, 154t, 154bl, 154br, 184t, 184b, 195t, 195b, 203b, 276t, 294t, 294b, 295t, 295c, 295b, 296b, 297

U.S. Army Military Institute, 160t, 160c, 160bl, 160br

U.S. Coast Guard, 233b, 234t, 234bl, 234br

U.S. Department of the Interior, 10t, 10c, 10b, 11t, 11b, 12, 13t, 13b, 18, 22b, 23t, 32, 33t, 33b, 38, 44t, 44b, 45t, 45bl, 45br, 51t, 51b, 52–53, 55b, 56–57, 59, 60t, 60b, 61b, 72t, 72c, 72b, 76, 77, 78–79, 86t, 86b, 87t, 88t, 88b, 89t, 91, 92t, 92b, 93b, 97b, 98–99, 100, 103t, 103b, 104cl, 104cr, 104bl, 107t, 110t, 110b, 112t, 119l, 121b, 122–23, 128b, 131t, 131bl, 131br, 134t, 140t, 144t, 144b, 156t, 156c, 156b, 162t, 162b, 163t, 163b, 167t, 167c, 167b, 169c, 169b, 170bl, 170br, 172t, 173t, 173ct, 173cb, 173bl, 173br, 176l, 176r, 177cl, 177cr, 177b, 193t, 193cl, 193cr, 193b, 197t, 197b, 198t, 201t, 202t, 202b, 207, 209, 217, 218t, 218b, 221t, 224, 225

U.S. Marine Corps, 236t, 236b, 237tl, 237tr, 237b, 256b, 288b, 289t, 289c, 289cr, 289bl

U.S. Navy, 243t, 243b, 246t, 246b

Vermont Travel Division, 185

VMI Museum, 196t, 196b

Wyoming State Archives and Historical Department, 223

INDEX